EDWIN M. BRIDGES

PROBLEM BASED LEARNING

FOR
ADMINISTRATORS

WITH THE ASSISTANCE OF
PHILIP HALLINGER

ERIC Clearinghouse on Educational Management
University of Oregon
1992

Library of Congress Cataloging-in-Publication Data

Bridges, Edwin M.
    Problem-based learning for administrators / Edwin M. Bridges ; with the assistance of Philip Hallinger.
        p.   cm.
    Includes bibliographical references.
    ISBN 0-86552-117-4 : $10.95
    1. School administrators—Training of—United States. 2. School principals—Training of—United States. 3. School management and organization—Study and teaching—United States. 4. Problem solving—Study and teaching. I. Hallinger, Philip, 1052-   .
II. Title.
LB1738.5.B75 1992
370'.7'6—dc20   92-71619
                                                       CIP

Design: LeeAnn August
Type: 10.5/12.5 Palatino
Printer: McNaughton-Gunn, Sabine, Michigan

Printed in the United States of America, 1992
Second printing, August 1993

ERIC Clearinghouse on Educational Management
  University of Oregon
  1787 Agate Street
  Eugene, OR 97403-5207
  Telephone: (503) 346-5043 Fax: (503) 346-2334

ERIC/CEM Accession Number: EA 023 722

This publication was prepared in part with funding from the Office of Educational Research and Improvement, U.S. Department of Education, under contract no. OERI-R 188062004. The opinions expressed in this report do not necessarily reflect the positions or policies of the Department of Education. No federal funds were used in the printing of this publication.

The University of Oregon is an equal opportunity, affirmative action institution committed to cultural diversity.

ii

MISSION OF ERIC
AND THE CLEARINGHOUSE

The Educational Resources Information Center (ERIC) is a national information system operated by the U.S. Department of Education. ERIC serves the educational community by disseminating research results and other resource information that can be used in developing more effective educational programs.

The ERIC Clearinghouse on Educational Management, one of several such units in the system, was established at the University of Oregon in 1966. The Clearinghouse and its companion units process research reports and journal articles for announcement in ERIC's index and abstract bulletins.

Research reports are announced in *Resources in Education* (*RIE*), available in many libraries and by subscription from the United States Government Printing Office, Washington, D.C. 20402-9371.

Most of the documents listed in *RIE* can be purchased through the ERIC Document Reproduction Service, operated by Cincinnati Bell Information Systems.

Journal articles are announced in *Current Index to Journals in Education. CIJE* is also available in many libraries and can be ordered from Oryx Press, 4041 North Central Avenue at Indian School, Suite 700, Phoenix, Arizona 85012. Semiannual cumulations can be ordered separately.

Besides processing documents and journal articles, the Clearinghouse prepares bibliographies, literature reviews, monographs, and other interpretive research studies on topics in its educational area.

CLEARINGHOUSE
NATIONAL ADVISORY BOARD

Jim Bencivenga, Education Editor, The Christian Science Monitor
Gordon Cawelti, Executive Director, Association for Supervision and Curriculum Development
Timothy J. Dyer, Executive Director, National Association of Secondary School Principals
Patrick Forsyth, Executive Director, University Council for Educational Administration
Joyce G. McCray, Executive Director, Council for American Private Education
Richard D. Miller, Executive Director, American Association of School Administrators
Samuel Sava, Executive Director, National Association of Elementary School Principals
Thomas Shannon, Executive Director, National School Boards Association
Don I. Tharpe, Executive Director, Association of School Business Officials International
Gene Wilhoit, Executive Director, National Association of State Boards of Education

ADMINISTRATIVE STAFF

Philip K. Piele, Professor and Director
Keith A. Acheson, Associate Director
Stuart C. Smith, Director of Publications

Dedication

To the eighteen participants in the Prospective Principals' Program who made this book a reality: Ellen Back, Paige Cisewski, Lyn Cornwall, Kit Cosgriff, Kathy Doi, Diane Fort, Lupe Garcia, Sal Gutierrez, Gail Heinrich, Michael Kass, Suzanne Kulp, Debbie McCleskey, John Michaelson, Chris Rich, Candace Simpson, Mary Smathers, Nicki Smith, Nancy Sullivan.

The names of the teachers and administrators that appear in the projects are fictitious.

About the Author

Edwin M. Bridges, Professor of Education at Stanford University, is a two-time recipient of the Excellence in Teaching Award in the Stanford School of Education. He recently was asked to prepare a statement about his views on teaching for the Centennial Edition of *Campus Reports*, a University publication. His statement appears below.

Although I find teaching intrinsically rewarding and filled with exciting intellectual challenges, I also recognize that my enthusiasm for teaching must be nurtured. To maintain a high level of interest in teaching, I rarely teach a topic or a course twice in the same way. My penchant for experimentation sometimes leads to disappointment; a lesson flops or an entire course goes awry. That is the price I willingly pay to sustain my passion for teaching.

My own conception of the teacher's role is influenced in large part by the fact that I teach in a professional school. As someone who prepares prospective principals, I feel obligated to create an instructional environment in which these future principals learn how to apply their newly acquired knowledge. Through my attempts to fulfill this obligation, I now understand how much I initially underestimated the difficulties inherent in applying knowledge to problems of practice. I continue to search for and experiment with instructional approaches that teach students how to use their knowledge appropriately and effectively.

One approach that I am developing and testing in my courses is problem-based learning. This instructional strategy has the following features: (1) the starting point for learning is a problem, (2) the problem is one that students are apt to face as future principals, (3) students are exposed to theory and research that are relevant to the problem, (4) students decide how to use this knowledge in solving the problem, and (5) most learning occurs within the context of small groups rather than lectures.

At the heart of teaching are views about the conditions under which students learn best. My own views lead me to emphasize the importance of creating a supportive classroom environment in which mistakes are regarded as learning opportunities and the instructor models the practices and philosophy that he espouses. I continually strive to infuse my teaching with these ideals.

Edwin M. Bridges
Professor of Education

Contents

Foreword

The ERIC Clearinghouse on Educational Management is pleased to make available to those who are responsible for training school principals this groundbreaking book on an innovative instructional strategy. Edwin M. Bridges, with the assistance of Philip Hallinger, offers a clearly written, multifaceted look at *problem-based learning*, an approach in which students, working together in small groups, take responsibility for solving problems they are apt to face as future professionals.

The reader will be happy to discover that these pages contain no abstract, theoretical speculation about how problem-based learning (PBL) might work but rather a firsthand account of how this strategy has been put to use in the Prospective Principals' Program at Stanford University. Those who are interested in implementing a similar program will save themselves many hours of frustration by paying attention to Professor Bridges' candid, balanced description of what worked and what didn't at Stanford. At the very least, the reader will come away from this book with a concrete understanding of what PBL is and convinced that it offers great promise for restructuring the ways in which principals are prepared for their positions.

This volume is the second title published by the Clearinghouse that Dr. Bridges has authored. *Managing the Incompetent Teacher*, first published in 1984 and revised in 1990, is one of our best-selling monographs and one that thousands of school district officials across the nation have used in implementing policies and procedures that ensure a high quality of teaching in their districts. We believe that

Problem-Based Learning for Administrators is destined to do for principal training what *Managing the Incompetent Teacher* has done for supervision and evaluation of teachers.

Dr. Bridges is a professor of education and director of the Prospective Principals' Program at Stanford University. Formerly Dr. Bridges served as director of the Midwest Administration Center at the University of Chicago. His current research focuses on problem-centered instructional strategies for preparing future administrators. Dr. Bridges has also written extensively on the practices used by school administrators in dealing with incompetent teachers, the problems of handling teacher absenteeism, and shared decision-making. His treatment of these problems appears in such journals as *The Administrative Science Quarterly, Educational Administration Quarterly*, and *Administrator's Notebook*.

Dr. Philip Hallinger is an associate professor of educational leadership and director, Center for the Advanced Study of Educational Leadership at Peabody College, Vanderbilt University. Formerly the director of a principals' training center, he is particularly interested in developing better methods of educating school leaders. He has recently coedited a book, *Cognitive Perspectives on Educational Leadership* (Teachers College Press, in press), and a forthcoming issue of *Educational Administration Quarterly* devoted to cognition and school administration.

Philip K. Piele
Professor and Director
ERIC Clearinghouse on Educational Management

Preface

During most of my professorial career, I have been interested in using problem-centered instructional strategies to prepare future administrators. Initially, my efforts concentrated on the case method and its handmaiden, discussion teaching. Later I dabbled with the case incident technique, which is a variant of the orthodox case method of teaching. More recently, I have experimented with problem-based learning.

For those who share my interest in problem-centered teaching strategies, I can recommend some valuable references for two of these methods. Christensen (1981) has written a comprehensive book about the case method; he, Garvin, and Sweet (1991) have edited a similarly useful book on discussion teaching. Pigors and Pigors (1980) have written the definitive book on the case incident process.

For those who are interested in exploring how problem-based learning (PBL) might be used to prepare administrators, I have written this book. Since problem-based learning is a relative newcomer to the field of administration, I discuss this instructional strategy from two perspectives, the conceptual and the operational. I have included three problem-based learning projects that might be used by those who choose to try this approach. Each of these projects has been field tested and revised in light of the results from the field tests.

To those who may be stimulated to experiment with problem-based learning, I wish you the same joy and renewed interest in teaching that I have experienced. Although it is the winter of my career, it feels like spring.

Acknowledgments

I am indebted to the following individuals for reading and commenting on an earlier draft of this book: Tom Chenoweth, Kenneth Hill, William S. Howe, Henry Levin, Philip Piele, Candace Simpson, Stuart Smith, and Decker Walker. Their suggestions stimulated me to stretch myself and to create a more readable book. They, of course, bear no responsibility for any weaknesses that may exist in the finished work. That responsibility falls on me.

I owe a special debt of gratitude to Philip Hallinger. He has contributed important ideas at all stages of the book's development and has provided valuable feedback on several drafts of the manuscript. In addition, Philip has played a significant role in refining and extending my initial conceptualization of how problem-based learning can be used to prepare administrators. The projects that he and his students have developed are, in my judgment, exemplary; the response of my students to these projects has been overwhelmingly positive.

Philip Hallinger and I wish to acknowledge the generous support of the Walter S. Johnson Foundation and the Danforth Foundation; these two foundations made our developmental work on problem-based learning possible.

Introduction

For the past five years Philip Hallinger and I have been actively involved in developing, field testing, and refining a new approach to preparing educational administrators: problem-based learning. In this book I chronicle what happened during this exciting and satisfying period of my professional life. Although I am highly enthusiastic about this instructional approach, I have tried to hold my enthusiasm in check and to write a balanced account of this innovation. Perhaps the reader will profit as much from my mistakes as my successes.

Whenever I discuss problem-based learning (PBL), two related questions commonly surface: How does PBL differ from the case-method and traditional instruction? What happens during a PBL class session? Anticipating these two questions, I take the reader inside three classrooms in chapter 1 and briefly describe how the topic of teacher selection might be introduced using traditional, case-method, and PBL approaches. In chapter 3, I detail how the instructor and a group of prospective principals actually dealt with this topic in a PBL classroom. These two accounts should provide the reader with a reasonably clear understanding of what problem-based learning is and how it operates in a classroom context.

To further aid the reader in understanding this instructional approach, I have included several examples of the instructional units that we developed for the problem-based learning component of the administrator preparation programs at Stanford and Vanderbilt Universities. We refer to these units as problem-based

1

learning *projects*. Three such projects appear in Appendix B. The ERIC Clearinghouse on Educational Management will publish these projects, along with others that we have developed, in a forthcoming series. To facilitate use of these projects, we intend to include teaching notes and reprints of the relevant reading materials.

Since problem-based learning changes the traditional role of students and instructors, I discuss several ways to ease the transition. In chapter 2, I focus on the students' role and how we minimize the frustration and difficulties they experience in the PBL curriculum at Stanford. Chapter 4 centers on the role of instructors in problem-based learning and how they may deal with the challenges that arise while implementing a PBL project. In chapter 6, I describe the obstacles that may hinder the implementation of PBL in a higher education context and outline a strategy for overcoming these impediments.

Potential users of problem-based learning understandably are interested in what students actually learn through this approach. Since this instructional strategy is in its infancy, my discussion of this important issue is impressionistic and illustrative. Immediately following my description of what happened during the PBL project on teacher selection in chapter 3, I discuss my impressions of what students learned and failed to learn about his topic. In chapter 5, I reproduce a number of student essays to illustrate what students report learning about leadership and a host of administrative skills. These essays also reveal how their newly acquired knowledge and attitudes relate to the rationale and design of a PBL curriculum.

Since this book represents a "first cut" on problem-based learning, the last chapter sketches an agenda for future research and development on problem-based learning. A few students and faculty have already begun working on this agenda, and they have experienced the same sense of intellectual challenge and fulfillment that I have.

Problem-Based Learning: Background and Rationale

Early in 1987 Larry Cuban, then associate dean of the Stanford University School of Education, and Mike Smith, dean, approached me about starting an M.A. program for prospective principals. Once I agreed, I proceeded to consult broadly with faculty and local administrators about how the program should be designed. The program that emerged is described in Appendix A.

During one of my discussions with faculty members, I became aware of problem-based learning (PBL). Richard Snow, a cognitive psychologist, provided me with a set of reading materials about this instructional approach and how it had been used to train physicians. After reading these materials, I became excited about the possibility of using a variant of this approach to prepare administrators.

My own thinking about PBL has been enriched by the work of Barrows (1984), the pioneer of this approach in medical education, and other medical educators. However, since my interest centers on preparing administrators, not physicians, I have created my own conceptualization of PBL for this purpose. Those who wish to explore how PBL has been used by medical educators should refer to the bibliography.

In this chapter I introduce my conceptualization of PBL by exploring three interrelated issues—the nature of problem-based learning, the rationale behind it, and the research on its effectiveness. Subsequent chapters provide the reader with ideas about how this instructional approach can be introduced to students, an example of how problem-based learning operates in a classroom setting, a description of the instructor's role, an indication of what students learn in a PBL environment, and suggestions for implementing PBL in a higher education context.

PBL: What Is It?

To begin our discussion of problem-based learning, let us step inside three classrooms and listen to the instructors as they introduce the topic of teacher selection.

Classroom 1: Traditional Instruction

Near the end of the class session, the instructor announces,

That concludes our discussion of teacher socialization. At our next meeting we will be discussing teacher selection. In line with previous class discussions, you should come prepared to discuss the readings listed in your course syllabus. I want you to pay particular attention to the readings about two selection methods—the interview and the work sample—and the paper that discusses research on the effectiveness of various selection tools. I would also like for you to think about how this material might be used to design a teacher selection process.

Classroom 2: Case Method of Instruction

Near the end of the class session, the instructor announces,

Before our next meeting, I want you to read the case, "Mr. Jones: A Case of Mistaken Identity." This case describes the selection process that the XYZ School District used when choosing Mr. Jones for an elementary teaching position and what happened during his first year on the job. School has been in session for five months, and it is now clear that Mr. Jones is unsuited for the position. Come to class prepared to discuss the following:

1. What are Mr. Jones's principal teaching strengths and weaknesses?

2. Why does Mr. Jones seem to be doing so poorly?

3. How would you change the district's selection process to increase the odds of choosing someone with the "right stuff"?

Be prepared to explain and justify your conclusions.

Classroom 3: Problem-Based Learning

Near the end of the class session, the instructor announces, "Your next project will be on the topic of teacher selection." (In chapter 3, I describe how this project actually unfolds in the classroom.)

While the instructor distributes copies of the project's description (a copy appears in Appendix B), he continues his comments:

You will have three class sessions (three hours each) to complete this project. Ellen has agreed to be the project leader. At the first session she will be assisted by Michael and Gail; he will be the recorder while she will act as the facilitator.

In this project, the team is constituted as a selection committee. You will design a selection process and implement it with three finalists. The three finalists, one novice and two experienced teachers, are candidates for an elementary teaching position. You have to decide which candidate will be recommended for the position. To assist you in designing the selection process, I have supplied a number of pertinent readings and guiding questions. If you look at the learning objectives in the project description, you will have a sense of what I expect you to learn from this experience.

As with previous projects, I will act as an observer and a resource to the team. You, of course, will decide how you are going to complete your committee's assignment and to accomplish the learning objectives. If you choose the right person for the job, you can spare yourself all the problems detailed in *The Incompetent Teacher*.

From the third example, we can see that problem-based learning (PBL) is an instructional strategy that has the following characteristics:

1. The starting point for learning is a problem (that is, a stimulus for which an individual lacks a ready response).

2. The problem is one that students are apt to face as future professionals.

3. The knowledge that students are expected to acquire during their professional training is organized around problems rather than the disciplines.

4. Students, individually and collectively, assume a major responsibility for their own instruction and learning.

5. Most of the learning occurs within the context of small groups rather than lectures.

There are two major versions of problem-based learning: problem-stimulated learning and student-centered learning (Waterman, Akmajian, and Kearny 1991). These two species of problem-based learning are defined primarily by the major goals of the curriculum and the extent to which the instructor or the student determines the learning objectives, the resources (for example, references and relevant experts), and the modes of evaluation for each focal problem within the curriculum. Up to this point, I have concentrated my efforts on explicating and using problem-stimulated learning.

Problem-Stimulated Learning

Problem-stimulated learning uses role relevant problems as "the means by which new knowledge is introduced and learned" (Waterman, Akmajian, and Kearny 1991, p. 8). This version of PBL emphasizes three major goals: (1) the development of administrative skills, (2) the development of problem-solving skills, and (3) the acquisition of the knowledge base that underlies administrative practice. To foster attainment of these principal learning goals, the instructional staff highly structures the learning materials for each focal problem in the curriculum. These learning materials include the following:

- an administrative problem

- a list of objectives that the student is expected to master while working on the problem

- a reference list of books, articles, and audiovisual materials that pertain to the basic objectives

- a series of questions that focus the student on important concepts and applications of the knowledge base

Students work with these learning materials as a project team. The team has a fixed period in which to complete the project, to resolve the problem, and to accomplish the learning objectives. The time allotted to each project varies from two to five three-hour sessions spread over a two-day to two-week period. During the life of the project, each student is assigned a particular role—leader, facilitator, recorder, or team member. The team schedules its own activities and decides how it will use the allotted time to solve the problem and master the learning objectives. Student performance is evaluated by instructors, peers, and self using a range of techniques—questionnaires, interviews, observation, and paper-and-pencil tests.

Instructors do not serve as dispensers of information. Rather, they serve as resources to the team and provide guidance and direction if the team solicits assistance or becomes bogged down as it works on the problem-based learning project.

Student-Centered Learning

Student-centered learning resembles and differs from problem-stimulated learning in several ways. Like problem-stimulated learning, student-centered learning begins with an administrative problem that introduces the student to a variety of learning issues. Similarly, students work on the problem in project teams with a faculty member who serves as a resource, rather than as a dispenser of information. Students in both versions of problem-based learning also are evaluated in multiple ways by instructors, peers, and self. The two approaches to problem-based learning further share two common goals: developing administrative and problem-solving skills, and building a knowledge base for administrative practice.

Unlike problem-stimulated learning, student-centered learning emphasizes the goal of fostering the skills needed for lifelong learning. To promote attainment of this goal, the instructor presents a problem; however, he or she specifies neither the content to be mastered nor the books, articles, and other resources to be consulted. Once the instructor presents the problem, students identify the learning issues they wish to explore and proceed to locate and read materials that pertain to their self-defined learning issues. As with problem-stimulated learning, students decide how they will use the newly acquired knowledge in dealing with the problem.

PBL: Why Use It?

My own interest in exploring the potential of PBL in preparing administrators rests on cognitive, motivational, and functional grounds. In the paragraphs that follow, I elaborate on these three grounds; they constitute my rationale for embarking on the quest to formulate a problem-based learning strategy for preparing educational administrators.

Cognitive Grounds

Problem-based learning has been used extensively in the field of medicine to train future physicians (Jonas, Etzel, and Barzansky 1989). The rationale for using this approach rests in part on four propositions that, in my judgment, apply with equal force to the preparation of administrators.

1. Students retain little of what they learn when taught in a traditional lecture format (Bok 1989).

2. Students often do not appropriately use the knowledge they have learned (Schmidt 1983).

3. Since students forget much of what is learned or use their knowledge inappropriately, instructors should create conditions that optimize retrieval and appropriate use of the knowledge in future professional practice.

4. PBL creates the three conditions that information theory links to subsequent retrieval and appropriate use of new information (Schmidt 1983): activation of prior knowledge, similarity of contexts in which information is learned and later applied, and opportunity to elaborate on that information.

Prior knowledge is activated; that is, students apply knowledge they already possess in order to understand the new information.

This prior knowledge and the kind of cognitive structure in which it is stored determine what is understood from the new experience and what is learned from it. Problems are selected and sequenced to ensure that this activation of prior knowledge occurs.

The context in which information is learned resembles the context in which it will later be applied (referred to as encoding specificity). Research shows that knowledge is much more likely to be remembered or recalled in the context in which it was originally learned (Godden and Baddeley 1975). Encoding specificity in problem-based learning is achieved by having students acquire knowledge in a functional context, that is, in a context containing problems that closely resemble the problems they will encounter later in their professional careers.

> The advantage of such an approach is that students become much more aware of how the knowledge they are acquiring can be put to use. Adopting a problem-solving mentality, even when it is marginally appropriate, reinforces the notion that the knowledge is useful for achieving particular goals. Students are not being asked to store information away; they see how it works in certain situations which increases the accessibility. (Prawat 1989, p. 18)

Information is better understood, processed, and recalled if students have an opportunity to elaborate on that information. Elaborations provide redundancy in the memory structure, which in turn reduces forgetting and abets retrieval. Elaboration occurs in problem-based learning in various ways, namely, discussing the subject matter with other students, teaching peers what they first learned themselves, exchanging views about how the information applies to the problem they are seeking to solve, and preparing essays about what they have learned while seeking to solve the problem.

Motivational Grounds

According to one major theory of motivation, the effort that people are willing to expend on a task is a product of two factors (Good and Brophy 1991). One factor is the degree to which they *expect* to be able to perform the task successfully if they apply themselves, and the other is the degree to which they *value* the rewards that successful performance will bring (Good and Brophy). In line with the tenets of *expectancy theory*, instructors should use motivational strategies that address these factors. Furthermore, instructors should create the preconditions that are essential to the effectiveness of any motivational strategy (Good and Brophy).

In several ways, problem-based learning strives to create the **essential preconditions** for successfully using motivational strategies. The instructor creates a *supportive learning environment* by encouraging students to take risks, by praising students for their risk-taking attempts, and by treating mistakes and "failures" as learning opportunities. The instructor assigns tasks at the *appropriate level of difficulty*. This precondition is achieved by choosing projects that are neither too easy nor too difficult for the student and by gradually increasing the complexity of each project. The instructor chooses each PBL project with *meaningful learning objectives* in mind. If the project is problem-stimulated, the instructor identifies what the objectives are and explains to students in an introduction to the project why the objectives are worth mastering. Finally, the instructor uses *a variety of strategies* to stimulate student motivation. The variety of motivational strategies used in PBL are discussed later in this section.

To maintain students' **expectation of success** in a PBL instructional environment, the instructor underscores how the curriculum has been designed to promote success. Projects have been chosen and sequenced in such a way that students will acquire the basic skills they will need to succeed in this instructional environment. Moreover, each problem-stimulated project contains a knowledge base and a set of guiding questions that may prove helpful to students as they attempt to deal with the focal problem. Finally, students are encouraged to draw on other resources to assist them in thinking through the problem. Each successful completion of a PBL project strengthens the expectation that effort leads to success.

To underscore **the value** of learning activities in a PBL curriculum, instructors may use extrinsic or intrinsic motivation strategies. An extrinsic motivation strategy links task performance to consequences that students value. These consequences may take one of several forms: rewards for good performance, instrumental value in achieving future success, and rewards achieved through competition with others. In a PBL environment, the instrumental value of learning activities is emphasized. Each PBL project contains an explicit rationale that explains why the project was included in the curriculum. The rationale also discusses how the knowledge and skills that are emphasized in the project relate to the future responsibilities of the administrator.

Intrinsic motivation strategies are based on the idea that students will expend effort on tasks and activities they find inherently enjoyable and interesting even when there are no extrinsic incentives. Each PBL project contains six elements that most students, according to Good and Brophy, find enjoyable or intrinsically rewarding.

1. *Provides opportunities for active response.* In each PBL project students learn by doing something. They engage in a wide array of activities—leading, recording, discussing, facilitating, making decisions, developing and revising schedules, making oral presentations, holding conferences, and the like.

2. *Includes higher-level objectives and divergent questions.* At the heart of each PBL project are a problem to be solved, a situation to be analyzed, knowledge to be applied, alternatives to be evaluated, and consequences to be forecast. All these tasks involve higher-order intellectual skills. The hallmark of PBL is applying knowledge, not simply recalling it.

3. *Includes simulations.* In a PBL instructional environment, the instructor incorporates simulations into most PBL projects. For example, students participate in mock meetings of a board of education and a superintendent's cabinet. Students also role play conferences, handle inbasket items, and conduct classroom observations by viewing videotapes of classroom teaching episodes.

4. *Provides immediate feedback.* In a PBL environment, instructors position themselves to observe students and how they are using or misusing the knowledge they are attempting to master. When it becomes clear that students either do not understand a particular concept or are unable to use it appropriately, the instructor can supply immediate feedback.

5. *Provides an opportunity to create finished products.* Most PBL projects conclude with a product (for example, a memo to the superintendent or a classroom observation report), a performance (such as a postobservation conference with a teacher or an oral presentation to a board of education), or both. These products challenge students and heighten their level of concern.

6. *Provides an opportunity to interact with peers.* Since the basic unit of instruction is a project and students work as members of a project team, students interact extensively with peers. Every stu-

dent has a role on the project team and participates actively in accomplishing the project's objectives. The person occupying the project facilitator role is responsible for ensuring that all team members are actively involved in the team meetings and that no one dominates the discussions.

Functional Grounds

In an earlier paper (Bridges 1977), I analyzed the work of a student and the work of an administrator along four dimensions: the rhythm of the work, the hierarchical nature of the work, the character of work-related communications, and the role of emotions in work. Based on this analysis, I concluded that there is a major dysjunction between the work of a student and the work of an administrator. I also contended that this dysjunction may result in trained incapacity; in essence, to paraphrase Kenneth Burke (1935), the student "becomes unfit by being fit for an unfit fitness."

Problem-based learning narrows the gap between the work of a student and the work of an administrator in several ways; therefore, it is more likely to result in trained capacity rather than trained incapacity.

With respect to the *rhythm of the work,* the tempo of a student's work in a PBL environment more closely corresponds to the accelerated work pace of the administrator than does the work of a student in a conventional instructional environment. Students work under time constraints to complete a problem-based learning project, and the time available is rarely sufficient. Moreover, the modes of thought and action that students use in a PBL environment differ from those that students use in conventional instruction. Time deadlines in the PBL environment force students to balance the need to understand (that is, analyze) with the need to act. Since they are judged on the feasibility of their actions, as well as the thoroughness of their analysis, they are less likely to become victims of "analysis paralysis."

The *hierarchical nature of the work* of a student in a PBL environment also more closely resembles the work of an administrator. In a conventional instructional environment, students occupy subordinate roles. Their work is largely individualistic and competitive; the deficiencies of "fellow employees" enhance rather than diminish their standing in the workplace. The student's work in a PBL environment is strikingly different. Students serve as team leaders, facilitators, and members of a project team. Through these experiences, students come to appreciate the dependency inherent in managerial roles, the necessity of delegating responsibilities to others, and the difficulties and frustrations inherent in trying to obtain results through other adults.

The *character of work-related communications* contrasts sharply in PBL and conventional instructional environments. In conventional instructional environments students spend most of their time in receiving roles, they rely heavily on the written mode of communication using the impersonal language and the detached style of the academician, and they engage in one-way communication. The character of work-related communication in a PBL environment more closely resembles those of the administrator. PBL students, like administrators, spend roughly equal amounts of time in sending and receiving roles, rely heavily on oral modes of communication, prepare written memos (the dominant form of written communication for administrators), and work in small face-to-face interpersonal settings that are conducive to two-way communication.

The *role of emotions in work* also is quite different in the two types of instructional environments. In a conventional instructional environment students work in a relatively placid emotional climate. Ideas, not feelings, are the currency of the realm. Affective neutrality is the dominant expressive state as it is congruent with the contemplative and scientific character of academic work. In a PBL environment, the emotional tone of the interpersonal environment is more varied and jagged. Students, like the administrators they aspire to be, encounter the emotional problems of working with people. These occasions create opportunities for students to test their competence in interpreting and responding to the feelings of others. When projects go awry, students also acquire insights into how they deal with frustration, anger, and disappointment.

PBL: What Difference Does It Make?

The effectiveness of problem-based learning in preparing professionals for their future roles has been studied most extensively in the context of training future physicians. After reviewing the focus and results of this research, my interest in exploring the potential of this approach in preparing administrators persisted despite the fact that the review revealed a few unexpected results.

Focus

The vast majority of research on problem-based learning focuses on a variant of the following question: *Do problem-based learning programs produce better outcomes for medical students than do traditional programs?* The major outcomes of interest in descending order of investigation are (1) student attitudes toward the instructional environment, (2) knowledge of the basic disciplines represented in medical curricula, (3) clinical competence, (4) approaches to studying, (5) career preferences, (6) completion time and rates, and (7) study loads. Regardless of the outcomes being studied, most of this research fails to specify what species of PBL is being compared to the traditional program.

A small set of studies focuses on nonstudent outcomes. These studies investigate one of the following issues: instructors' motives for teaching in a problem-based learning program (Wilkerson and Maxwell 1988), costs of PBL versus traditional programs (Mennin and Martinez-Burrola 1986), students' preferences for PBL or traditional programs (Jones and others 1984, Kaufman and others 1989), and the correspondence between faculty and student perceptions of learning needs in a problem-based program (Shahabudin 1987).

Results

Compared with traditional programs in medical education, PBL yields superior or equivalent results on all but one of the outcome measures studied (see table 1).

Students in the PBL programs express substantially more positive attitudes toward their training than do students in more traditional programs. The former are inclined to praise their training, especially those aspects that are unique to problem-based learning, whereas the latter are more likely to describe their training as boring, irrelevant, and anxiety-provoking (deVries, Schmidt, and deGraaff 1989 and Schmidt, Dauphinee, and Patel 1987).

TABLE 1

Problem-Based Learning in Medical Education:
Summary of Research

Basic research question: Do PBL programs produce better outcomes for students than traditional programs?

Outcomes Studied	*Results*
1. Attitudes toward the instructional environment	1. PBL substantially more positive.
2. Approaches to studying	2. PBL students adopt meaning orientation (desirable outcome); traditional students adopt reproducing orientation.
3. Career preferences	3. PBL students more likely to become primary physicians (desirable); traditional students become specialists.
4. Completion time and rates	4. PBL students complete in less time and at higher rate than traditional students.
5. Knowledge of basic disciplines	5. Small differences favor traditional programs, but PBL students show steeper growth during period of study.
6. Clinical competence	6. Small differences favor students in PBL programs.
7. Study loads	7. No major differences.
8. Self-directed learning skills	8. Not investigated.

Besides expressing more positive attitudes toward their training, students in PBL programs also adopt more desirable approaches to studying than their traditional program counterparts. Students in traditional programs are more likely to adopt a *reproducing orientation* to studying, that is, use rote learning and seek to reproduce the factual information in the syllabus. PBL students, on the other hand, are more likely to adopt a *meaning orientation*, that is, to be intrinsically motivated by the subject matter and to strive to understand the material (Coles 1985; deVolder and deGrave 1989; Schmidt, Dauphinee, and Patel). Moreover, PBL students seem to expend an equal, if not greater, amount of time and effort on their studies (deVries, Schmidt, and deGraaff).

In countries with relatively high dropout rates among medical students, there appear to be noticeable differences in the completion times and rates of PBL and traditional students. PBL students in Holland are much more likely to graduate and to do so in less time than students in the more traditional schools (deVries, Schmidt, and deGraaff 1989).

Upon graduation from medical school, PBL students apparently pursue different careers in the field of medicine than do graduates of traditional programs. The most pronounced tendency is for PBL graduates to choose family medicine and practice more often than graduates of traditional programs. This tendency was evident in three of the four studies that investigated career preferences of medical graduates (deVries, Schmidt, and deGraaff; Kaufman and others; and Schmidt, Dauphinee, and Patel).

When I examined the research related to the major goals of medical education, the results were somewhat surprising. In light of the cognitive rationale advanced for PBL, I had expected results that clearly favored students in PBL programs. The results did not match my expectations, however. On tests of medical knowledge, students in the traditional programs scored higher than students in the PBL programs, but the differences were small (Schmidt and others; deVries, Schmidt, and deGraaff; and Kaufman and others).

More in line with my expectations were the results of some recent work completed by Bransford and others (1989). This research indicates that learners who acquire information in the context of problem solving are much more likely to use it spontaneously to solve new problems than are individuals who acquire the same information under conventional fact-oriented learning conditions.

The clinical competence of PBL students is better than that of their counterparts in traditional programs, but the differences are small and nonsignificant. This pattern holds true for problem-solving proficiency and performance of students during the clerk-ship, residency, and internship phases of their medical training (deVries, Schmidt, and deGraaff; Jones and others 1984; Kaufman and others; and Schmidt, Dauphinee, and Patel).

Since researchers have not investigated differences in the self-directed learning skills of students in PBL and traditional pro-grams, I can reach no conclusions about differential attainments of this educational goal.

In light of the widespread concern about rising medical costs, I was further surprised to find only one study that focused on the costs of PBL and traditional programs. Costs were studied exclusively in terms of the time instructors spent on teaching. There were no differences in the *amount of time* spent on teaching; how-ever, there were substantial differences in *how instructors spent their time*. In the PBL track, instructors spent 72 percent of their time in contact with students and 28 percent in preparation for this contact. The reverse was true in the traditional track, where instructors spent 61 percent of their time in preparation and only 39 percent in contact with students (Mennin and Martinez-Burrola).

Summary

Problem-based learning is an instructional strategy that uses a problem as the starting point for learning. The problem is one that students are apt to face as future professionals. The knowledge students are expected to acquire during their training is organized around problems rather than the disciplines. Students work in project teams on these problems and assume a major responsibility for their own instruction and learning.

The two most common species of PBL are problem-stimulated and student-centered learning. Both versions emphasize three major learning goals: (1) the development of administrative skills, (2) the development of problem-solving skills, and (3) the acquisition of the knowledge base that underlies administrative practice. These two versions of PBL differ primarily in the importance attached to the goal of lifelong learning and the extent to which the instructor defines the learning objectives, resources, and modes of assessment. Problem-stimulated learning attaches less importance to the goal of lifelong learning and is more highly structured by the instructor than student-centered learning.

Thus far, Philip Hallinger and I have concentrated our efforts on explicating and using problem-stimulated learning. This instructional strategy creates the conditions that optimize the retrieval and appropriate use of formal knowledge in future professional practice. It also increases students' motivation by programming them for success and by using an array of extrinsic and intrinsic motivational strategies. Furthermore, the work of a student in a PBL instructional environment more closely resembles the work of an administrator than it does in conventional instruction. As a result, PBL students should be somewhat better prepared to handle the work of an administrator.

The effectiveness of PBL in preparing professionals for their future roles has been studied extensively in the field of medical education. Compared with traditional programs for training physicians, PBL programs yield superior or equivalent results on all but one of the outcomes studied.

Introducing Problem-Based Learning to Students

Students often encounter difficulty in making the transition from a traditional to a problem-based learning environment. Medical educators have alluded to these difficulties, and we have observed them as we have worked with aspiring and practicing administrators. By properly attending to these transitional issues, instructors can reduce the frustration experienced by students and can accelerate their successful adjustment to this instructional approach.

To ease the students' transition to a PBL environment, instructors may use three different, but complementary, approaches. First, they can provide students with an orientation to this instructional approach prior to their commencing on the PBL projects that form the core of problem-based learning. Second, instructors can rely on problem-stimulated, rather than student-centered, projects during the introductory phase of PBL. Finally, instructors can facilitate students' adjustment to PBL through the choice and sequencing of projects. In this chapter, I discuss each of these approaches.

Orienting Students to PBL

Prior to their initial encounter with PBL, I have found it helpful to provide students with an overview of this instructional approach. This overview is organized around the questions that students commonly ask about this approach. The questions I pose and the answers I provide are the subject of the paragraphs that follow. The overview builds on and extends the discussion of PBL presented in the first chapter.

What Is Problem-Based Learning?

Problem-based learning is an instructional strategy that organizes knowledge around administrative problems rather than the disciplines. There are two major versions of PBL: problem-stimulated and student-centered learning. In both versions, students work on these problems as members of a project team. These features of problem-based learning are detailed in chapter 1.

What Is the Rationale Underlying PBL?

There are cognitive, motivational, and functional grounds for using PBL as an instructional strategy in preparing administrators. Moreover, there is a substantial body of research that attests to the value of using PBL in training future professionals. The grounds and the research evidence are discussed at length in the first chapter.

What Are the Major Goals of PBL?

Four major goals lie at the heart of problem-based learning: (1) acquisition of the knowledge base underlying administrative practice, (2) development of administrative skills, (3) development of problem-solving skills, and (4) development of lifelong learning skills. The problem-stimulated version of PBL stresses the first three goals, while the student-centered version emphasizes all four.

What Is a PBL Project?

A problem-based learning project is the basic unit of instruction in a PBL curriculum. The features of a PBL project depend upon whether it is a problem-stimulated or a student-centered

TABLE 2

Features of Problem-Stimulated and Student-Centered PBL Projects

Features	Problem-Stimulated Projects	Student-Centered Projects
Introduction	X	X
Problem	X	X
Learning objectives	X	
Resources	X	
Product specifications	X	X
Guiding questions	X	
Assessment exercises	X	
Time constraints	X	X

project. The features of each project type are listed in table 2 and discussed in the paragraphs that follow.

1. *An introduction.* This component introduces the student to the focal problem for the project and provides a rationale for including the problem in the curriculum.

2. *Problem.* Each project is structured around a high impact problem that the administrator is apt to face in the future. A high impact problem is one that has the potential to affect large numbers of people for an extended period. Some of these problems are highly structured, while others are complex, messy, and ill-defined.

3. *Learning objectives.* These objectives, limited in number, signal what knowledge and skills the student is expected to acquire during the project.

4. *Resources.* For each project, the student receives one or more of the following resources: books, articles, films, and consultants

(professors or practicing administrators). The specific nature of the resources depends upon the learning objectives and the problem that is the focal point of the project. Students are also encouraged to exploit the resources that exist in their own school districts.

5. *Product specifications.* Each project culminates with some type of performance (for example, oral presentation), product (such as a memo), or both. The specifications spell out what should be included in the performance or the product. To make these projects as realistic as possible, the product specifications are frequently ambiguous. This ambiguity creates some of the risk and uncertainty that are inherent in any project; moreover, the ambiguity affords students some leeway (the amount varies from one project to another) in defining the problem and attacking it.

Project management, like administration, seldom resembles drawing pictures by following the dots. Accordingly, prospective administrators need to learn how to function effectively when product specifications are unclear and how to cope with the psychological discomfort that often accompanies such uncertainty.

6. *Guiding questions.* Two types of guiding questions may be provided with the project. One type directs students to key concepts; the other type assists students in thinking through the problem.

7. *Assessment exercises.* Assessment takes several forms. Each project contains a "Talk Back" sheet that invites students to offer suggestions for improving the project (see chapter 6 for an example). In addition, students are encouraged to prepare an essay that reflects what they have learned during the project. (Numerous examples appear in chapter 5.) Occasionally, the project contains a "Knowledge Review Test" that enables them to check their understanding of key concepts.

8. *Time constraints.* Most projects are designed to last from two to five sessions; each session is three hours long. Projects terminate when the learning and product objectives are achieved. The clock is a constant enemy in problem-based learning projects. Team members find themselves continually struggling with the dilemma that confronts every conscientious manager, namely, how to achieve some reasonably high level of performance within severe time constraints. Managing this dilemma requires participants to make difficult choices and to set priorities (such as family versus work, quantity versus quality of output, and learning objectives versus

product objectives). Moreover, the dilemma underscores the need to work efficiently and to adopt time-saving measures.

These features of problem-based learning projects should become even clearer as the reader peruses the description of the field test of the project on teacher selection in chapter 3 and examines the other sample problem-stimulated learning projects in Appendix B.

How Are Project Teams Organized?

Each project team consists of five to seven students. Each student is assigned one of the following roles: project leader, facilitator, recorder, and team member. Students rotate roles from one project to another so that each student will have the opportunity to play all these roles.

Each team may be organized vertically or horizontally. If the team is organized vertically, the leader makes the crucial decisions when the entire team is unable to reach consensus. If the team is organized horizontally, majority vote is used to make crucial decisions when the entire team is unable to reach consensus.

When sufficient numbers of students are available, the composition of the teams changes from one project to the next. Since the composition of each team, the leader, and the duration of the project may vary across projects, students become exposed to the situational nature of leadership and the risk and uncertainty that are characteristic of managerial work.

What Is the Role of Students in a PBL Project?

Students play an extremely active role in a PBL project. They, not the instructor, shoulder the responsibility for what happens during the life of a project. The leader and other team members are responsible for figuring out how the project objectives will be accomplished, on time, with the available resources.

Team members should not lose sight of the fact that each project has dual objectives. One set relates to the *learning objectives*—the knowledge and skills participants are expected to acquire during the life of the project. The other set relates to the *product objectives*—the resolution of the problematic situation that lies at the heart of problem-based learning. There is the ever-present danger that team members will become consumed with trying to accomplish the product objectives and will slight the learning objectives in the process. The leader and other team members are responsible for seeing that both objectives of the project are accomplished.

(Important as these dual results are, they represent a myopic view of results that must be achieved through people. Even though a project team may have successfully accomplished its learning and product objectives, it may have been a miserable or frustrating group experience. Team members who have unpleasant group experiences are likely to have little appetite for working together in the future. When a project leads to frustration, this becomes an occasion for reflecting on what went wrong and why.)

If the project is problem-stimulated, students have little discretion over what the learning objectives and resources will be. Team members are expected to become familiar with the knowledge contained in the resources that have been included with the project. However, they decide how and whether the knowledge that has been provided will be used to deal with the problem. In the real world, people consult various sources for ideas and advice when they are confronted with a problem and use those that seem most relevant and consistent with their own values. The same condition generally prevails in the problem-based learning projects.

If students are assigned to a student-centered project, they are afforded somewhat greater discretion than in a problem-stimulated project. They are further empowered to choose what their learning objectives will be and what resources they will read or consult.

How Are Students Evaluated?

Students are evaluated primarily for the purpose of promoting personal and professional growth. Three sources of evaluation are used to accomplish this purpose—self, peer, and instructor. Formative evaluation is based primarily on the student's performance at team meetings, the student's or team's final product and/or performance, and the student's mastery of the learning objectives. Feedback is oral as well as written, underscores what the student is doing especially well, and highlights some things for the student to think about or consider in relation to his or her performance.

Students also receive a summative evaluation at the end of the quarter in the form of a pass/no credit. Students do not fail (that is, receive no credit) unless they have ample forewarning that this may occur. Thus far, all students have received a "pass."

Another question students commonly ask about PBL—What is the role of the instructor?—is addressed in chapter 4.

Using Problem-Stimulated Learning Projects

As a second way of easing the transition of students to a problem-based learning environment, the instructor may use problem-stimulated, rather than student-centered, learning. By adopting the more structured approach, the instructor can reduce student frustration, speed up the learning process, and increase the chances that students will experience success.

A student who has received extensive exposure to PBL at Stanford explains how and why this occurs in a problem-stimulated learning format. Her explanation is reprinted in the sidebar on pages 26 and 27.

Choosing the Contents and Sequence of the Projects

The students' transition to problem-based learning may also be eased by the instructor's choice and sequencing of the problem-stimulated learning projects. During the introductory phase of the Stanford PBL curriculum, students participate in five problem-stimulated projects. These projects emphasize a set of skills that enable students to succeed in a PBL instructional environment, namely, skills in meeting management, problem framing, written communication, oral communication, and time management. (For

Student Perspective on the Value of Problem-Stimulated Learning

Dear Ed:

You asked me to jot down some of my thoughts about the relative merits of student-centered and problem-stimulated learning in a program like the Prospective Principals' Program. Here are a few completely subjective ideas....

I am sure that you will not be surprised to hear that I can list many advantages for the PPP model [essentially, problem-stimulated learning], mostly deriving from the focus provided for participants' effort. Specifically, the "clothes" provided for the problem assist learning in the following ways:

- *The learning objectives* identify and prioritize skills and knowledge relevant to school administration.

- *The guiding questions*
    - prevent wild-goose chases due to misidentification of central issues.
    - signal what is important to know.
    - identify theoretical frameworks relevant to the problem.

- *The resources*
    - provide necessary background in disciplines relevant to the problem.
    - focus attention on high quality materials.

- *The product specifications* introduce different ways of collaborating, delegating responsibilities, and presenting solutions.

The model also motivates participants by providing psychological support for the learner. Specifically, the materials provided with the problem statement:

- prevent frustration over wasted time
- reduce uncertainty about how to proceed
- increase the chance of success in managing a complex problem
- are straightforward and nonmanipulative in stating what is to be learned and what is expected of participants.

The overall model [problem-stimulated] inculcates a value for treating induction into a professional group as an assisted learning process....

For all these reasons, I believe the additional assistance provided by the problem-stimulated model is more appropriate for administrator training. Learning this process has been as important as achieving the learning objectives of the projects. I believe that long association with this model in the program has enabled PPP participants to assimilate it and use it skillfully in their work lives. I doubt that we would have developed our group leadership and problem-solving skills as effectively or quickly had we been required to invent such a model.

—Candace Simpson, Coordinator of Human Resources, Palo Alto Unified School District, Palo Alto, California

a summary of these projects, see the sidebar on page 28.) These skills are some of the same ones they will need as administrators.

In line with the theory underlying problem-based learning, we have sought to create a spiral curriculum. We consciously sequence these five projects so that each successive project draws on the knowledge and skills developed in preceding projects. The spiraling character of this curriculum provides students with repeated opportunities to practice and refine their skills. From the students' vantage point, this is one of the best features of the problem-based curriculum that we have created.

Summary

Since students encounter difficulty in making the transition to a problem-based learning environment, instructors should consciously strive to make this transition a smooth and successful one. I have endeavored to discuss three complementary approaches an instructor may use to accomplish this objective. Instructors may provide students with an extended overview of problem-based learning. Instructors may also rely on highly structured problem-stimulated learning projects during the introductory phase of a PBL curriculum. Finally, instructors may select projects that provide students with the basic skills they will be using in the problem-based learning environment. If the projects are sequenced in a spiral fashion, students will have repeated opportunities to practice and perfect these skills. Consequently, students are more likely to exploit their learning opportunities fully and to experience success in the process.

Summary of Problem-Stimulated Projects in the Introductory Phase of a PBL Curriculum

Meeting Management. Students learn to run meetings using the Interaction Method. After reading about this method, they use it to deal with the "desert survival" problem. We chose a noneducational problem because we wanted participants to focus on issues of process, not content. Students are expected to use this method in managing the meetings of future projects.

Problem Framing. During this project, students learn about problem definition and acquire a strategy for attacking "wild" problems, problems that are ill-defined, complex, multifaceted, and ambiguous. Students use their newly acquired knowledge to deal with three problems—two at the classroom level and one at the school level. Each succeeding problem is more difficult and complex than its predecessor. As students encounter "wild" problems in future projects, they draw on the knowledge and skills acquired during this project.

Write Right! Students read about a reader-centered approach to written communication and a system for editing memos. They use these methods to prepare a memo to the superintendent about a messy situation ("wild" problem) that exists at their school. Nearly half of the parents in a first-grade classroom have kept their children home for one day and have threatened to boycott the classroom indefinitely. Students use these two methods in subsequent projects to prepare their written communications.

Present Your Case! Students learn how to make persuasive informational oral presentations. The project centers around a controversial issue—how to incorporate AIDS education into the high school curriculum. Participants present their recommendation and rationale orally to a three-member board of education (role played by current and former board members). Students use these presentational skills in subsequent projects that involve oral presentations.

It's About Time! During this project, students participate in a two-hour simulation involving a range of activities and problems—handling correspondence, dealing with interruptions, conducting a classroom observation, holding an unscheduled meeting with a hostile parent, handling a phone call from an irate parent, and making an oral presentation to a faculty committee. Following the simulation, students establish a set of priorities for the school and develop a strategy to ensure that they have time to pursue their priorities. In choosing these priorities, students draw on the background material about the school and the problems that they have encountered in the simulation.

Problem-Based Learning in the Classroom: An Example

The Stanford University Program for Prospective Principals includes three six-unit courses that use problem-based learning as the main instructional strategy. The basic unit of instruction in these three courses is a problem-stimulated learning project; each course consists of a series of such projects.

In this chapter I describe what happened during the field test of the project on teacher selection. I pay particular attention to four aspects of this project: (1) how I set the stage for this project, (2) what transpired during the four three-hour class sessions devoted to it, (3) how the participants reacted to what happened, and (4) what they and I learned from the experience. In preparing this account, I have relied on videotapes of three sessions, minutes prepared by team members, essays written by participants at the conclusion of the project, and copies of the participants' final products.

Setting the Stage

Five days prior to the first class session devoted to this project, I provided participants with a nine-page description of the project and a packet of reading materials. (The revised project description appears in Appendix B.) In addition, I assigned the fourteen class members to either an elementary or a high school selection committee depending upon their level of interest. I further designated one person in each group as the committee chair for the life of the project and identified who would serve as the facilitator and recorder for each class session. (Participants had learned about these roles in a previous project on meeting management.) The occupants of the facilitator and recorder roles rotated from one session to another.

I then provided each committee with the names, phone numbers, and addresses of the three people who would act as candidates in the group's selection process. The candidates for the high school vacancy were students in Stanford's Teacher Education Program who volunteered for the project, knowing that they, too, would benefit from the experience. Finally, I announced that the project should be completed within three class sessions (three hours each). (Later I extended the length of the project by one session and asked each committee to reserve the last thirty minutes of the final session for a joint debriefing.)

To simulate the major features of the selection process, I charged each selection committee with the following tasks:

1. Develop a set of criteria for evaluating the applications and use these criteria to screen the applications provided with the project.

2. Design an interview and work sample.

3. Use the interview and work sample to decide which of the three candidates will be recommended for the position.

4. Notify each "applicant" of the outcome and offer suggestions for improvement to those who were not chosen.

5. Prepare a one-page report to the personnel director. (This report should contain the committee's recommendation, an overview of the selection process, a justification for its recommendation, and a plan for ensuring the candidate's success once hired.)

To assist each committee in completing its tasks, I supplied members with some guiding questions and a number of references on relevant issues such as recruitment, the legal aspects of selection, the treatment of beginning teachers, and the validity of various selection tools. In addition, I furnished them with a set of learning objectives to underscore what they were expected to learn while completing these tasks.

In the account that follows, I describe what happened during each of the four class sessions and note my thoughts and reactions to what I observed. For the most part, my description centers on what transpired in the elementary selection committee. This particular committee was composed of seven participants in the Prospective Principals' Program; they ranged in age from thirty-four to forty-six. Six of these participants were female (two Asian-Americans, one African-American, and three whites). The seventh was a white male who had just completed two years as the acting principal of a small middle school.

Act I

(First session of project: 1:15-4:05)

(Note: Three days prior to the first meeting of the selection committee, the chair [project leader] distributed a memo to the six members of the committee. In this memo, the chair indicates that she has skimmed the resource materials for the project and proposes a division of labor for completing the reading assignments. She encourages the group to read the materials with the intent of finding the parts that will be helpful to the committee in completing its tasks. She further encourages each committee member to read the description of the project, the background information, and the description of the Redwood City School District. Finally, the chair foreshadows what will happen at the first meeting, namely, share the reading material, decide on the criteria to be used when screening the applications, and complete the paper screening.)

Scene 1 (sixteen minutes)

The chair opens the meeting by distributing a copy of the revised agenda (see table 3). She proceeds to review the agenda. When she reaches the last item on the day's agenda, she says, "We may not have time to complete the paper screening phase. I checked with Ed, and he said that we could omit this phase if we run short of time." One member responds, "I hope we don't have to drop it." Another nods her head in agreement.

T A B L E 3

Agenda for First Session

Group: Practicum 422
Date: July 9, 1991
Starting time: 1:15 p.m.
Ending time: 4:05 p.m.

Project II

Order of Agenda Items	Person(s) Responsible	Process	Time
Introduction	Ellen	overview	15 min
Review reading material	Kathy	pairs/jigsaw	40 min
School description questions	Kathy	pose	20 min
Create guidelines for interview & sample lesson	Kathy	brainstorm	20 min
Break			10 min
Develop criteria for paper screening	Kathy	brainstorm checkerboard	45 min

.... [Tentative agendas for next two sessions.]

When she completes her review of the agenda, she solicits questions and suggestions. Only two questions are raised: (1) "In what form will we provide feedback to the three candidates for the position?" (Question unresolved.) (2) "Has anyone been involved in the teacher selection process?" Two members respond "Yes" and proceed to describe the nature of their experiences.

During this entire discussion, I remain silent. I note to myself that the committee chair has invested a lot of time and thought into planning the entire project and is extremely well organized. The other members appear attentive throughout the discussion, and the project apparently has started smoothly.

Scene 2 (sixty minutes)

The facilitator identifies herself and proceeds to describe the process that will be followed in reviewing the reading material for the project. "In phase 1 we will meet in pairs to share what we have learned from the readings that Ellen assigned us. When phase 1 is completed, one person from each of the three pairs will meet together to discuss what they have learned about each of these topics."

Following the facilitator's brief description of this process, the students immediately move into phase 1. The chair of the selection committee circulates among the three pairs but does not actively participate in the discussion. I position myself to observe the pair discussing the research. Since each student has read the same material, the discussion centers around the highlights of the readings and how the material is relevant to one or more of the committee's assigned tasks. I think to myself that they have read the material thoroughly, understand the basic concepts, and recognize the relevance of these concepts for the selection process. Their verbal exchange is balanced; no one dominates the discussion. Neither student asks me a question nor attempts to draw me into the discussion. They seem to be oblivious to my presence and the video camera that is taping their discussion. When they finish, they look for the facilitator and signal that they are ready to move to phase 2. The other two pairs finish a few minutes later.

Sensing that everyone has completed phase 1, the facilitator moves to the front of the room and asks the group to form two triads with each triad containing one member of each pair. The students waste no time forming their triads, and the chair joins the triad consisting of Michael, Nancy, and Gail. I decide to spend my time observing this foursome.

Each member of the triad takes a turn discussing what he or she has read. I note that the students listen intently to each presentation, write comments on the summary provided by the presenter, and offer additional insights if they have also read the material. Students freely discuss their views about the importance of what they have read and occasionally urge their peers to read a reference that they have found especially useful. They underscore their opinions by saying things like, "This is an absolute must." Since I had admonished students to elaborate on how the knowledge might be applied to the selection problem, I am anxious to learn if they follow my advice. I am not disappointed. In each instance the student states explicitly how the reference can be used in this situation or in some future selection decision.

During this sixty-minute discussion, I make only four comments. On one occasion I offer some gratuitous information about the person who had authored the paper on work samples. Later I volunteer the information that two of the candidates for the position are experienced while the other is a novice looking for a teaching position. At one point I encourage the students to talk with Dr. H., a staff member, as he is being sued for a negative recommendation of a former employee. Only once do I find it necessary to intervene for purposes of clarifying a concept that everyone has difficulty grasping.

Scene 3 (twenty-five minutes)

Instead of moving to the next scheduled agenda item, the facilitator states,

> I have some doubts about the decision to divide the committee into two subgroups to work separately on designing the work sample and the interview. After listening to the discussions about these two selection tools, I believe that it will be much more difficult to design an interview than a work sample. I think that the entire committee should be involved in designing the interview.

In the discussion that follows, committee members begin to raise other issues that trouble them. What criteria will be used to screen the applications? Will the same criteria be used to evaluate the work sample and the interview? Should the committee delay the screening of applications until the end of the project and complete this activity only if there is time? None of these issues is resolved.

During this discussion, one group member asks me to comment on the extent to which school districts use the same or different criteria when screening and interviewing applicants. I respond briefly:

> The personnel process in most districts lacks coherence among its various parts. The criteria for evaluating teachers are seldom reflected in the hiring process; moreover, each component of the selection process isn't tightly and explicitly linked to the other parts of the process. I hope that you will recognize the value of designing a process that has more unity and coherence than exists in most districts.

(*Note* : Months later while reviewing this tape I recognize that I should have provided the facilitator with feedback about her behavior during this discussion. At the time I became too involved in the content of the discussion and inadvertently abandoned my observer-feedback role. Consequently, I missed the opportunity to make the facilitator aware of how she might have dealt with her reservations about the process for designing the interview without sidetracking the discussion.)

Intermission (ten minutes)

Scene 4 (thirty-five minutes)

The facilitator stands at the front of the room and begins to discuss the next item on the agenda. Although the agenda designates the item as "developing a school description," the task is somewhat broader. She announces that the group will be generating a description of the district, the school, and the job for which the candidates are applying. To complete the task, the facilitator recommends a two-step process: "I suggest that we adopt the perspective of a candidate and ask questions that a candidate is likely to have about the district, the school, and the job. Then we can decide on the answers that we will provide to these questions." While the facilitator describes the content and the process for the discussion, the recorder attaches three long sheets of butcher paper to the chalkboard. At the top of each sheet she writes one of the following words: district, school, and job.

For the next thirty minutes the committee follows the process suggested by the facilitator. The group generates a list of questions under each of the headings: district, school, and job. Although the group's discussion never strays from the task, it is much more lighthearted than the one before the break. When the group completes its lists of questions, the facilitator moves from question to question, inviting committee members to suggest a possible answer. In supplying answers to the questions, committee members draw from various sources—their own experience, the background information provided for the case, and recent courses, especially the one taught by Hank Levin on the "Accelerated School." The group enthusiastically endorses someone's suggestion to portray the school as one that is transforming itself into an Accelerated School and the principal as one who uses a style of shared leadership.

During this discussion I merely act as a nonparticipant observer. I take notes on what is happening and think about what I want to highlight later in the debriefing.

Scene 5 (seventeen minutes)

Once the group has completed its description of the district, school, and job, the facilitator moves to the next item on the agenda. She invites the group to list alternative uses for this information. The group spends most of its time using the information to brainstorm a set of criteria for judging the paper screening and interview. Although the group has not finished this activity, the leader intervenes and says, "Let's stop now and resume this discussion on Thursday. In the time remaining, let's decide what information we will give to the applicants and agree on the things that need to be done before the next meeting."

Rushed for time, the group makes decisions in rapid-fire fashion. The recorder volunteers to take the butcher paper home and type up the notes. Someone else suggests the agenda for the next meeting: decide on the criteria, complete the paper screening, and design the work sample and the interview. Another member raises the possibility of not doing the work sample. I quickly reply, "You really don't have an option on the work sample; you have to do that."

Scene 6 (debriefing; ten minutes)

During the debriefing I share several perceptions about the process. I praise the leader for her organization of the session and the entire project. I also share my perception that the group became frustrated during the discussion just before the break. Almost in the same breath, I add that this frustration was not evident during the second half of the session when there was a much more positive tone in the group. My discussion of the process concludes by commending the group for integrating concepts from Hank Levin's class into the selection project.

I also share some views about the contents of their discussion concerning the issue of criteria:

> In my judgment, your list of possible criteria contains apples and oranges. Some relate to the requirements of the job; others relate to the experience and qualifications of the applicants. I hope that the group will give more thought to this issue. The message of the readings underscores the need to focus on what you want the candidate to do once hired and to design a selection process that enables you to determine whether the candidates can and will do what is expected of them.

I close by saying that I am tempted to redesign the selection project to encourage students to do as they have done. "You seemed to enjoy generating the description of the district, school, and the job. Did I misread it?" The group acknowledges that the activity had been enjoyable and allowed them to draw on their experience.

One member talks about how shifting the group activity after the break also seemed to defuse the conflict between the leader and one of the group members. Recalling this episode, I add that the group leader was, after she overcame her initial block, able to adjust her plan in light of the suggestions made by N— , a group member. I praise the leader for her adaptability and acknowledge how difficult it was for her to modify the plan because she had invested so much time and effort into it. The session ends, several minutes past the scheduled time.

Act II

(Second session of project: 1:05-4:15)

Scene 1 (seventy minutes)

The leader opens the meeting with a brief overview of the day's agenda and immediately turns the meeting over to the facilitator. She remains seated and states that the recorder will be Michael, who is standing at the chalkboard next to several strips of butcher paper that he has taped to the board. She then introduces the first item on the agenda: brainstorming a list of criteria to be used in evaluating the applicants.

Although the group eventually agrees on its criteria (see table 4), there is a great deal of wheel-spinning. The discussion wanders frequently off course, and I note mounting frustration. On one occasion, I enter the discussion to note that the content of the discussion is unclear and cite several examples of the different topics being discussed. The facilitator responds by keeping the content of the discussion in focus. As I observe the group once again begin to flounder, I volunteer another comment, this time about process: "Your process seems confusing to me. You seem to be brainstorming, evaluating, and rewriting the criteria—all at the same time. N— (the facilitator), I think you should clarify what process is being used and follow it. That would probably help the group accomplish more."

Although the facilitator attends more explicitly to issues of content and process, I think to myself that the discussion is less productive than it might be. Just before the break, I say:

> The group is still experiencing some problems related to the content and the process of the discussion. This may be due to N—'s playing two roles—managing the discussion and participating fully as a group member. I think the group might experience fewer problems if she concentrates on managing the content and process of the discussion and abandons her role as group participant.

One of the group members immediately follows my suggestion with one of her own: "I think N— (the facilitator) should stand during the discussion. That would further differentiate her role from the rest of the group."

TABLE 4

Selection Criteria

These criteria were provided to candidates several days prior to the interview and work sample.

You will be evaluated on the following criteria during the work sample (W) and/or during the interview (I), as determined by evidence that you can

— choose from and demonstrate competence in a variety of teaching strategies (W)

— communicate effectively (I,W)

— communicate in a language other than English, preferably Spanish (I)

— create a positive, supportive learning environment (I,W)

— demonstrate successful classroom management skills (I)

— demonstrate understanding of the "Accelerated Schools" philosophy (I)

— design a lesson integrating two or more subject areas (W)

— modify lessons to meet the needs of students (I,W)

— participate collaboratively (I)—plan and present an effective lesson (W)

.............[twenty criteria in all]

Intermission (ten minutes)

Scene 2 (twenty-two minutes)

The facilitator resumes the discussion by asking, "What do you want to do with the information (list of criteria) we just generated?" The group easily agrees on the task and proceeds to designate for each criterion whether it will be used to judge the interview, work sample, or both. During the discussion the facilitator stands and keeps the group on task. Whenever someone strays from the agreed-upon content or process, she immediately refocuses the group. Occasionally, she signals that she is stepping out of her facilitator role to offer a suggestion or opinion about the content. Whenever the group disagrees about whether a criterion should be assessed by means of the interview or the work sample, she asks group members to state the reasons for their choices. If the group is unable to resolve the issue, she asks group members to declare their preferences. The facilitator rarely resorts to voting, because group members usually agree to use both methods after hearing each person's reasons for preferring the interview or the work sample.

Scene 3 (four minutes)

The facilitator signals that the group now faces several choices. She asks the group, "Should we work together or divide into two groups to design the work sample and interview? Or, would you prefer to complete the paper screening?" After hearing one another's views on these issues, the group easily reaches agreement. It decides to work together on designing the work sample and the interview in that order.

Scene 4 (twenty-seven minutes)

The group defines its task as developing guidelines for the work sample and constructing a scoring system. Without much disagreement, the group develops the work sample guidelines around the following topics:

Content: fifth-grade lesson on fractions that integrates math and language arts.

Length: fifteen minutes.

Composition of class: low achievers; 45 percent Hispanic, 45 percent Anglo, and 10 percent Other.

Lesson plan: to be written and seven copies provided to the committee, one for each member.

Criteria: a list of the criteria that will be used to assess the candidate's performance in the work sample.

I enter this discussion at only one point. Someone asks, "Should we tell them the criteria?" I immediately respond "Yes" and justify my response on the grounds of fairness:

> Most districts that use a work sample judge it on the basis of Madeline Hunter's lesson planning model. In none of the districts that we have studied does a district announce its criteria. Candidates with inside information know what the criteria are and have a distinct advantage in the selection process. To create a level playing field, everyone should know what the criteria are.

To focus the discussion on the scoring system, the facilitator suggests one option and solicits others. The group quickly settles on three options: two-point scale (a criterion is either met or not met), a three-point scale (high, medium, or low performance on a criterion), and a two-point scale with comments noted about particular strengths. The facilitator moderates a discussion on the merits of each option and then polls the group. Everybody prefers a two-point scale with comments noting especially strong performance.

Scene 5 (twenty-five minutes)

While the recorder tapes additional sheets of butcher paper on the chalkboard, the facilitator introduces the next item on the agenda. She indicates that the group must decide on its interview questions and develop a scoring system. Under the direction of the facilitator, the group suggests how the discussion of the interview should proceed. The facilitator reframes the suggestions as options and asks the group members to indicate which option they prefer. With little or no disagreement, the group chooses to construct five broad questions and to indicate which criteria are being used to assess the candidate's responses. These questions appear in table 5.

TABLE 5

Teacher Selection—Interview

Interview Questions:

1. Please tell us about your background. What special skills and experiences do you bring to this position, in particular as they relate to our plans to become an Accelerated School?

2. How would you create a positive, supportive learning environment? Describe your system of classroom management.

3. How would you modify the lesson you gave today to meet the needs of a child with limited English proficiency?

4. What role do you think collaboration should play in teaching and learning? Please give examples.

5. Describe various kinds of assessment techniques you have used and how you have applied them in different curricular areas.

While discussing these five questions, the group also makes two other decisions. It decides to schedule each interview immediately following the work sample. By choosing this order, during the interview the group can probe how the candidate might modify the lesson to meet the needs of a child with limited English proficiency. The group also rejects a suggestion to provide each candidate with an opportunity to ask questions at the end of the interview. One member strongly opposes this possibility, and no one else speaks in favor of it.

The group quickly decides how to score responses to the interview questions. Using the relevant criteria, each committee member will use the same system being used to score the work sample—two-point scale plus comments. During this brief discussion, the recorder announces, "I have to leave promptly at 4:05 to pick up my son."

Scene 6 (eight minutes)

Recognizing that little time remains, the leader asks the group to deal with logistical matters. She states, "We need to agree on who will write up the notes from this meeting, what information we will provide each applicant, and who will phone the applicants and take the information to them." The recorder quickly volunteers to do everything, and three others offer to assist him. He asks for guidance from the group about what information to include in the packet that he will deliver to each applicant. The group immediately generates a list: information about the job, school, and district; information about the Accelerated School; the list of criteria; and the guidelines for preparing the work sample. He agrees to assemble this information and expresses some reservations about the number of criteria. "Personally, I find the list overwhelming." Someone else concurs. Although I also believe that the list of criteria is much too long, I decide not to press the issue because the group appears unwilling to pare the list.

Scene 7 (debriefing; two minutes)

Sensing the time pressure, I comment on only one issue. I probe to find out if M— was upset when I declared emphatically that the group had to use a work sample during the selection process. He replies, "Not at all." The meeting concludes. (*Note*: Later as I reflect on the session, I realize that I had failed to commend the facilitator for her performance after the break. She had changed her behavior, and the group had become much more productive. I vow not to repeat this mistake in future debriefings.)

Backstage: Following this session, the leaders of both committees approach me about the possibility of adding one session to the project. Both express strong feelings about this issue, and I accede to their request. At the outset of the project, I privately harbored some doubts about whether I had allowed sufficient time to complete it. The leaders' request validated my initial reservations.

Act III

(Third session of project: 1:15-4:05)

Today is "Selection Day." Each selection committee, having designed its selection process, now proceeds to implement it with three applicants for the position. I decide to change my pattern of remaining with the elementary committee for the entire session. I observe some portion of each committee's selection process and, along with Ken Hill, another staff member, interview each candidate following her appearance before the selection committee. We ask each applicant the following hypothetical question: "If you were offered the position, would you accept it based on how you were treated during the selection process?"

While observing the two committees, I note two main differences in how they are implementing their selection process. The secondary committee, unlike its elementary counterpart, has not required its candidates to teach a demonstration lesson. Instead, the secondary committee has incorporated a form of work sample into the interview.

The secondary committee has asked each applicant to plan a three- to five-day mini-unit for a sophomore English literature class on the theme Coming of Age and to bring a copy of this unit to the interview. During the interview, the committee asks each candidate to describe her lesson plan for the mini-unit. Following the presentation, the committee asks several questions related to the lesson plan, namely:

1. How did you go about planning this mini-unit? What resources did you use? What steps did you take?

2. You are in the middle of teaching this mini-unit and you feel it is going well. You are sitting in the teacher's lounge and you overhear two minority students, who are two of your strongest students, say: "This is so boring. Why do we need to know this? Is she from some other planet or something?" What would you do?

3. What strategies would you use to address the needs of limited English proficient students?

4. How do the writing activities you selected for your mini-unit improve the writing skills of your students?

When I discover what has occurred in the secondary selection committee, I decide on two courses of action. In the revised version of this project, I will stipulate that the work sample must involve teaching a demonstration lesson. This had been my intent all along, but my discussion of the work sample in the project description left open the possibility for other interpretations. My other decision relates to the debriefing at the conclusion of the project. During this activity I will invite the members of the elementary committee to comment on the value of a demonstration lesson in the selection process.

I also note that the climate differs in the two selection committees. The atmosphere in the secondary selection committee seems informal and relaxed while the tone of the elementary committee appears somewhat more formal and businesslike. These differences are evident during the opening and closing phases of the selection process, as well as during the interview and work sample phases. I wonder if these differences will affect the applicants' willingness to accept the position if it is offered. At the same time I decide to comment on the climate issue during the debriefing if the students do not raise it.

After this session, I reflect on what has transpired. The secondary selection committee's decision not to require its applicants to teach a lesson underscores one of the difficulties that can arise when the instructor works with more than one group. When an instructor works with several groups simultaneously, it is important to check the pulse of all the groups. I resolve in the future to devote more effort during and outside class to monitor what is happening within the project teams. If I had performed the monitoring function, I could have intervened and encouraged the committee to develop guidelines for a work sample that involved teaching a demonstration lesson.

Act IV

(Fourth session of project: 1:15-4:05)

During this final session of the teacher selection project, I once again move back and forth between the two committees.

Scene 1 (sixty-five minutes)

The leader of the elementary committee reviews the day's agenda and turns the meeting over to the facilitator. She announces the task confronting the elementary committee, "We have to reach consensus on whom to recommend. Let's begin by reviewing the strengths and weaknesses of each candidate."

One member immediately begins to enumerate the shortcomings of one of the candidates; others quickly follow suit. They agree that the candidate exhibited the following weaknesses during her demonstration lesson:

The objective of the lesson was unclear.

She ineffectively checked to see if we understood the material; all she did was ask whether we understood it.

She wasn't adequately prepared; midway through the lesson she introduced a word problem that she created on the spot.

She didn't pace the lesson well. Some of us finished the activities before others did; she had nothing for us to do. That runs the risk of behavior problems and too much time off task.

She never related the material to real life; there weren't any examples students can relate to.

Her vocabulary was too sophisticated for this age group.

Her diction and grammar were appalling.

At this point the facilitator says, "Don't forget that we have to provide her with feedback. Is there anything we can call a strength?" There is an extended pause. Finally, someone comments, "During the interview she seemed eager to take advantage of opportunities for professional growth and development. Maybe we could encourage her to do this." Another committee member says, "Let's commend her for her work in multicultural environments and her experience with children who have special needs."

I note to myself that the committee has strong, negative views about this candidate. Although I concur with their assessment of the candidate's shortcomings during the work sample, I am surprised by the depth and intensity of their feelings. In this instance, the committee has no doubts about the wisdom of its decision to reject the candidate. Based on the evidence, I judge the decision to be a reasonable one.

When the discussion shifts to the other two candidates, I observe some notable differences. The discussion is much less intense and clear-cut. Moreover, the committee members are drawing on the information from both the interview and the work sample. I am impressed that they continue to place considerably more weight on what the candidates can and will do than on matters of personal chemistry.

After thoroughly reviewing each candidate's performance during the work sample and the interview, the committee realizes that the two candidates seem fairly comparable. At this point it begins to consider the perceived strengths and weaknesses of both candidates simultaneously. The committee agrees that the two candidates demonstrated similar strengths during the work sample; for example, both presented well-organized lessons, used a variety of teaching strategies, used age-appropriate vocabulary and concepts, and showed an obvious concern for and sensitivity to students. Each candidate also revealed a weakness; one exhibited low energy during her lesson while the other relied on note cards.

Having compared the two candidates' performance in the work sample, the committee turns to the interview. During this discussion one member observes, "Both candidates lacked strategies for dealing with LEP (limited-English-speaking) students." The other committee members nod their heads in agreement. After a brief pause, another committee member states:

> When we asked the question about the Accelerated School, Paula displayed a lot more enthusiasm for working in this type of school than the other candidate did. She also highlighted the strengths she would bring to it. That, along with her strong interest in collaboration, really distinguishes her from the other candidate. I think we should hire her.

One member after another expresses support for this point of view. They look at one another obviously pleased, even a bit surprised, that they have made the decision without resorting to a formal vote.

The committee's decision, like so many selection decisions, ultimately involved a choice between two fairly comparable candidates. Neither candidate was clearly superior to the other; both possessed weaknesses as well as strengths. The committee's resolution to this relatively common choice situation seems reasonable and defensible in light of the evidence and its criteria.

Scene 2 (fifteen minutes)

Immediately following this agenda item the leader assigns committee members to one of two groups. The members of one group prepare the feedback that the committee will provide to each of the candidates, while the other drafts the memo to the superintendent. The committee members move into their assigned groups, and I spend a few minutes observing each group. I am pleased to see that the support plan for the recommended candidate addresses her principal teaching weakness, strategies for dealing with LEP students (see table 6). Moments later I leave the room and join the secondary committee.

Scene 3 (forty-five minutes)

The secondary group has just begun its debriefing. At the outset of this discussion I detect that the secondary group's experience has been somewhat less satisfying and educationally productive than the elementary group's experience. The secondary committee, unlike its elementary counterpart, had conducted the paper screening and chosen not to design a work sample that included a teaching demonstration. These two items consume most of the discussion.

The members express considerable dissatisfaction about the paper-screening phase of the project. Some of their concerns relate to the design of this phase:

"The materials were inconsistent."

"We needed a statement and recommendations as part of papers."

"Having paper for people we cannot really consider for interviews makes it a dead-end situation."

Other concerns relate to the group's own implementation:

"The protocol we developed was not very useful."

"We tried to come up with a process before looking at the papers."

"We shouldn't have used class time to screen; we should have screened them individually on our own time."

"We never had time to discuss our responses (to the screening phase); we had no idea why others thought the way they did."

TABLE 6

Memo from the Elementary Selection Committee to the Superintendent

To: Superintendent Smith

From: Teacher Selection Committee

Date: 7/23/91

Subject: Selection for fifth-grade teacher at Hank Levin Accelerated Elementary School

The committee recommends Paula Atwater for the position.

Selection Process:

- Created a job description.
- Developed "Can Do" criteria for candidate selection.
- Developed guidelines and protocols for work sample and interview.
- Distributed information to candidates.
- Observed work sample and conducted interview with each candidate.
- Reviewed strengths and weaknesses of each candidate.
- Selected a candidate by consensus.

Rationale:

1. Strengths as a classroom teacher
   - Uses a variety of teaching strategies to meet needs of all students
   - Demonstrates a child-centered approach
   - Creates a positive, supportive learning environment
2. Strengths as a collaborative team member
   - Displays enthusiasm for Accelerated School model
   - Has leadership experience (mentor teacher)
   - Works successfully with parents

Suggested Areas for Support:

- District orientation program
- Training: Accelerated School model Instructional Strategies for LEP students
- Peer coaching
- Observations and feedback

As for the work sample, their comments continue in somewhat the same vein. One person maintains, "The assignment needed more shape and definition." Most members refer to the process that the group used:

"We compromised what we learned from the resources."

"Frustrating to decide what to do and whether to use it."

"Participants in the interview question development group felt cut off from the work sample; there was no opportunity for input or revision. We didn't get to chew on the work sample."

Someone from the work sample group counters, "We felt you (the interview subgroup) wanted to redo what we had done."

"Our work sample was contrived and a compromise."

The discussion of the work sample then turns to what was learned. One person opines that she learned more than she had expected. Another comments, "I don't feel I learned much (from the work sample) because of the way we ended up doing it."

At this point the facilitator announces, "It is time to meet with the other committee for a debriefing." Everyone, including me, moves to the room where the elementary committee has been meeting.

Scene 4 (debriefing; thirty minutes)

The elementary and the secondary school selection committees meet together for the debriefing session. As the facilitator for the closing phase of this project, I invite the group to discuss two main issues. To introduce the first issue, I mention that the elementary selection committee, unlike its secondary counterpart, had asked the three candidates to teach a demonstration lesson to the committee. I then ask the members of the elementary selection committee to talk about the work sample that they designed and to discuss their reactions to the value of this work sample in their selection process. (Privately, I wonder what their reactions will be because several members of the committee seemed initially skeptical.)

The members of the selection committee proceed to discuss the features of their work sample, express their initial reservations about its value, and portray the work sample as "very valuable" and "tremendously worthwhile." After the first endorsement of the work sample, I ask if anyone holds a different view. None do; one after another they attest to the value of the work sample.

From time to time, members of the secondary selection committee ask questions about what happened during the demonstration lesson and probe to find reservations that the elementary group may not have expressed. One member of the elementary selection committee acknowledges, "I had considered the possibility that the work sample may have favored candidates who were stronger in the content area being sampled. Conceivably, the outcome might have been different if we had sampled a different content area." Another committee member says, "We had to make the assumption that the behavior was somewhat representative of each candidate's performance." Despite these concerns, everyone seems committed to using a work sample when selecting future teachers.

To introduce the second issue, I discuss the importance of designing a selection process with two objectives in mind: (1) to select the person with the "right stuff," and (2) to increase the likelihood that the preferred candidate will accept an offer. I then disclose that the three candidates for the secondary position had indicated to me that they would definitely accept the position if it were offered. However, all three of the candidates for the elementary position had expressed some doubts about whether they would accept an offer if it were forthcoming. In light of these differential outcomes, I invite the secondary group to comment on whether it had planned the selection process with the second objective in mind. If so, I further encourage the committee to discuss what it had done to accomplish this objective.

In the ensuing discussion, the members of the secondary selection committee underscore their conscious effort to treat their candidates humanely and describe how this objective permeated the committee's planning and subsequent treatment of the three applicants. Most committee members attribute their concern to the fact that the applicants were students in the Stanford Teacher Education Program. One member says, "I treated them just as I would if they were applicants for a position at a school where I was the principal." The members of the elementary selection committee listen attentively to the discussion but ask no questions.

Sensing that the discussion of this second issue has run its course, I inquire if anyone has a question that he or she would like to ask the other committee. Immediately, a member of the secondary committee says, "I am interested in knowing what the elementary committee liked about what it did to make its candidates feel at ease and what it might do differently."

Most of the elementary members contribute to the discussion that follows. One discusses the role of body language and how their actions during two of the interviews may have created problems for the candidate. Another talks about the awkward silence that occurred when the candidates completed their meeting with the committee. She acknowledges that the group just sat there until the candidates left the room. Still another raises the possibility that the committee may have overwhelmed the candidates with material to read and tasks to perform. One person highlights the actions that both committees apparently had in common.

At this point I realize what time it is and close the session.

Reactions of Participants

Although the elementary committee appeared to have a more positive experience with the teacher selection project than the secondary committee, the vast majority of participants, on balance, reacted favorably to the project. In the essays they prepared at its conclusion, participants summed up their sentiments as follows:

"Since I've never been formally involved in the selection process, this project was a definite must in terms of preparation for the principalship. It was extremely valuable to go through all the steps just as a practice and opportunity to gain information."

"Because I have seen the seamy side of teacher selection in the real world, I was very grateful for the chance to experiment with new approaches and simultaneously evaluate the process used in our district. I enjoyed the exercise of specifying a personalized support program as part of the recommendation to hire a new teacher. Why hadn't I thought of that? I will certainly try to incorporate this into the hiring process in my district."

"I found this project to be very practical and realistic."

"I am a convert to asking for work samples from teacher candidates.... We got a hands-on experience that I will not forget!"

"It was extremely valuable to read the reference materials and then try to apply what we had learned to creating protocols for the work sample and interview. Seeing a candidate in action in addition to reading about them and hearing them respond to questions is invaluable."

"I have seen how my district conducts interviews and now I know a much better model. Also, I wish to thank you for making this experience as real as possible by bringing in actual candidates. I could never have believed the value of a work sample had I not seen it myself."

"Talk about a paradigm shift! How useful it was to hear (at the end of our joint project debriefing) that none of our three candidates was interested in 'hiring on' with our group of folks. Only then did I realize what had happened during our project and what had, perhaps, gone wrong. We never once defined our task the way Ed did in our debriefing: to identify *and* to attract the very best candidate for the job."

"Reviewing the learning objectives for this project reminds me how little I knew at the outset except for having served on two selection committees in the P.V. School District. That practical experience coupled with this one, and the readings, have given me the knowledge necessary to design a selection process and the confidence to pull it off."

What Participants Learned

When participants complete a project, I usually am surprised by what they have learned. Some report learning about issues that I had not envisioned when I designed the project. Other participants learn much of what I had intended while some do not. The project on teacher selection is no exception. In this section I discuss my impressions of what participants learned during this project. I formed these impressions based on my observations of their meetings and my review of their products and integrative essays.

Unanticipated Learning Outcomes

In assigning participants to a selection committee that matched their grade-level interests, I mixed the participants from the second and third cohorts of the Prospective Principals' Program. For the first time participants found themselves working on a project team that consisted of people with whom they had not worked previously. In reflecting on this experience and the problems that ensued, most students commented about the importance of devoting time to team building when a new group forms. The leader of one group described his experience as follows:

> The contrasting styles of the second and third year participants were quickly apparent. We had assumed we shared the same agreements up front about the roles of leader, facilitator, and recorder, attitudes toward time, priorities of product versus learning as the objective of the experience, and attitudes toward conflict. Next time I will try to elicit agreements on these issues right away. I will work on team building and not assume it.

The leader of the other group, as well as most team members, echoed these same sentiments.

One participant learned what can happen when the facilitator enters the discussion as a participant and abandons her responsibility for managing the group process. While reflecting on her experience in this role, she wrote,

> One reason we did not do a teaching sample relates to one of the problems I saw us having as a group. We had one domineering group member who resisted compromise vehemently. Even when this person was a lone voice, she pushed her point of view hard until the rest of the group gave in somewhat. This person was strongly against having the candidates teach a lesson to us because it was unrealistic... I feel that the day and a half when I facilitated I was not strong enough in my facilitator role, putting a check on this person's control over the group. I contributed to the discussion too much and this distracted from my ability to take a neutral facilitator stance. I see more than ever the benefits of the non-participating facilitator."

Mission Accomplished

During this project I am reasonably confident that most, if not all, of the participants learned about a number of issues that I had designed into the project. They learned "how flawed and unreliable many selection tools are." Participants further gained insight into the role that personal chemistry plays during interviews and how to minimize its effect by the questions they ask. They also recognize that these questions should elicit what the applicant can and will do in terms of the criteria that are used to evaluate personnel once on the job.

Moreover, all seem to recognize that how candidates are treated during the selection process may influence their decision to accept a position if it is offered. In the words of one participant,

> In our combined debriefing we discussed the importance of attracting a candidate to the job. I'm glad this issue was raised because our group never discussed that.... I think any interviewing team should decide together in advance what they intend to do to attract teachers. This is probably omitted just as it was in our case. Again, learning by doing, particularly by making mistakes is the best way to learn.

Although this realization is an important one, I am less certain that participants know how to structure the selection process to increase the chances that the applicant will want to accept a job offer. In retrospect, I wish that I had explored this issue more directly during the debriefing. To assist future participants, I have added a reference on how to use the employment interview as a recruitment device.

Finally, participants understand how principals can create conditions that support or undermine the beginning teacher's classroom effectiveness. However, if these future principals do not subsequently use this knowledge to create more favorable working conditions for beginning teachers, I would judge the increased understanding to be of limited value.

Mixed Results

The members of the elementary selection committee appeared to have learned more about the work sample than did the members of the secondary committee. Based on my observations of the elementary committee's meetings and products, I am reasonably confident that its members know the guidelines to be followed when designing a work sample and are able to apply this knowledge; moreover, they are strongly committed to using a work sample in the selection process.

My sense of the secondary committee is that its members know the guidelines to be followed and understand how its own work sample failed to meet these guidelines. As one member candidly stated in her essay, "What I learned from the resources about the work sample was very valuable, even though our committee didn't use much of it: the fidelity of the task, the need for communicating clear criteria to the candidates, and the value of consistency in the conditions under which the work sample is produced."

Some members of this committee also became more receptive to the possibility of using the work sample after listening to the joint debriefing at the end of the project. However, for me to be convinced that the group knows and can use its knowledge to design a work sample, I would need to see the group actually designing another selection process. Until then, I remain skeptical that the members of the secondary committee can apply the knowledge they learned about work samples.

Indeterminate Outcomes

Although the participants reviewed the legal aspects of teacher selection and assignment, I am less clear than I should be about what they learned and how they might apply this knowledge. In my list of guiding questions for the project, I encouraged them to deal with this issue by asking, "What are the legal aspects of selection that may enter into this project?" During the discussions I observed, committee members did not discuss this issue.

To encourage future participants to grapple more with the legal issues, I revised the charge of the selection committee. The new version of the project requires each committee to develop a legally defensible application form and set of interview questions for the position.

Concluding Thoughts

Despite the generally positive reactions to this project, I realize that it, like most project premieres, has not been an unqualified success. Although the elementary committee found the project enjoyable and educationally worthwhile, the secondary committee encountered more frustration than I had anticipated and certainly desired. Moreover, in my judgment the learning objectives were not fully realized.

The somewhat disappointing experience of the secondary committee was due, in part, to the original design of the project. The information that I had provided about applicants during the screening phase was insufficient, and it was not integrated with the interview and work-sample phases. My instructions about the work sample also were ambiguous. This ambiguity, combined with the resistance of some students to designing a work sample that involved teaching a lesson, led to disappointing outcomes from both the students' and my points of view.

This field trial also underscored one of the difficulties inherent in managing more than one problem-based learning project at the same time. During the early stages of this project, I had devoted all of my attention to the elementary group and had ignored what was happening in the secondary selection committee. If I had monitored how the group was approaching its tasks, perhaps I could have eliminated or minimized the effects of the problems that surfaced in this committee.

Although I desire an unqualified success when students first try a project, that seldom happens. More commonly, I discover what the imperfections are and use this knowledge to improve the project. Since the revisions run much more smoothly, I am confident that the next version of the teacher selection project will lead to a more satisfying and educationally productive experience for everyone.

Role of the Instructor
in Problem-Based Learning

Duoring our preceding discussion of how problem-based learning operates in the classroom, we provided some insight into the role played by the instructor in a PBL project. In this chapter we move beyond this concrete example to consider the types of role-related activities that instructors engage in when implementing PBL projects. We also identify some of the major challenges that arise during implementation and discuss how the instructor may deal with them.

Role-Related Activities

The role of the instructor in a PBL environment can be defined in terms of what the instructor does not do, as well as what the instructor does. As our classroom example in chapter 3 shows, PBL instructors do not act as dispensers of knowledge, they do not conduct recitations, they seldom guide the discussion, and they generally do not manage the activities that occur during class time. In conventional classrooms, the two-thirds rule has become an iron law; two-thirds of the time someone will be talking and two-thirds of this talking will be done by the instructor. This rule does not apply to PBL classrooms, where the instructor talks substantially less than students. They, not the instructor, are the dominant participants.

PBL instructors engage in quite different activities. To further our understanding of these role-related activities, let's examine what instructors do prior to, during, and following a problem-based learning project.

Prior

Prior to assigning a project, the instructor engages in three main activities. First, he or she provides the students with an overview of PBL if students are unfamiliar with this approach. Second, the instructor assembles the resources, materials, supplies, and equipment needed to implement the project. To facilitate this activity, I have found it helpful to use a checklist; one appears in Appendix C. Third, the instructor assigns roles (leader, facilitator, and recorder) to the various members of the project team.

During

During the life of a project, the instructor engages in one or more of the following activities. He or she *observes the patterns of participation* along three dimensions: content, process, and frequency. *Content* refers to what is being said; it reveals whether students understand and are able to apply the knowledge to which they are being exposed. *Process* relates to who is talking, the tone of their comments, and how their comments fit into and contribute to the discussion. *Frequency* refers to whether the student's participation is relatively high or low. A useful discussion of how the instructor may observe the pattern of participation in a team discussion appears in the paper by Hertenstein (1991); I strongly recommend this paper to those who wish to sharpen their observational skills.

The instructor also *evaluates* the participation with a view toward facilitating the personal and professional growth of participants. In carrying out this activity, I endeavor to communicate the following:

1. "Here's what I observed...."

2. "Here's why it concerns (or impresses) me...."

3. "Do you see it the same way?..."

4. "If so, how might you do that differently in the future, or how might you try to deal with that concern?"

Despite my conscious attempt to follow these guidelines, I occasionally find myself skipping the last two.

The instructor may need to *intervene* if he or she observes that students are bogged down and spinning their wheels. The instructor may intervene by asking a timely question, by sharing perceptions of what seems to be happening and checking to see if students share these perceptions, and by offering to make suggestions about how the team may improve its functioning.

During a project, the instructor may also be called upon to *serve as a resource* to the team. In this capacity, the instructor responds to requests from students. They may want the instructor to clarify the meaning of obscure concepts, to answer questions that were stimulated by the project, to demonstrate skills, and to assist them in securing additional resources such as expertise or equipment.

The instructor *encourages* students to take risks and *supports* their efforts to do so. Some students lack self-confidence, so the instructor must consciously strive to create a nonthreatening, supportive environment where students feel comfortable in taking risks and overcoming their fear of failure. Instructors can create this kind of environment by providing high levels of positive feedback and by defining "failures" as learning opportunities.

As a project unfolds, instructors may need to *modify* it. These midcourse corrections may take one of several forms. If the instructor has not allowed sufficient time for the team to complete a project, he or she may either extend the length of the project or reduce the demands inherent in the product specifications. The instructor may also need to add key resources to the project in midstream. As students begin to work on a project, the instructor may recognize that they lack certain key skills and knowledge and may respond by adding resources that address these gaps. Instructors, as well as students, need to be flexible in a PBL environment.

Finally, the instructor may *conduct a debriefing* during the final phase of a problem-based learning project. These debriefings may center on what students learned during the project. Debriefings may provide project teams with an opportunity to share how they handled the focal problem of the project and why they dealt with it that way. Debriefings may focus on particular aspects of a project that strike the instructor as worthy of further discussion. For example, in the teacher selection project, I chose to limit the debriefing to discussing the work sample and the importance of designing a selection process to attract the preferred candidate.

Following

At the end of each project, the instructor ordinarily completes three main activities. First, he or she solicits feedback from students about their reactions to the project and how it might be improved. A form (referred to as "Talk Back") for obtaining this feedback appears in chapter 6. Second, the instructor provides written feedback to the students about their individual and/or group product and performance. Finally, the instructor reviews the students' comments on the project and uses this feedback to revise and improve it.

When providing written feedback to students, we endeavor to supply feedback that has the following characteristics:

- is neutral to positive in tone
- provides a balanced picture of strengths and weaknesses
- limits the number of concerns that are identified
- offers suggestions for dealing with the areas in need of improvement
- discusses the reasoning behind the suggestions
- poses questions for further reflection by students.

Students rarely receive this level of detailed, supportive, and constructive feedback; they deeply appreciate it when instructors take the time to provide it.

Major Challenges

In a PBL context, the instructor confronts a variety of challenges; let's look at what some of these challenges are and how an instructor may deal with them.

Students may experience difficulty in treating knowledge as a tool. In classroom settings, they are accustomed to summarizing what they have read and unaccustomed to considering how knowledge might be applied. As a result, they are likely to deliver "mini-lectures" to one another about the contents of what they have read. When this happens, the instructor may reiterate the importance of viewing knowledge as a tool and ask questions like the following: How might the knowledge in the readings be used in interpreting or understanding the problem? in solving the problem? in anticipating future consequences? in understanding the constraints or the opportunities associated with the problem? Alternatively, the instructor might ask if the knowledge in the readings raised any issues or questions that seem important for the team to consider in relation to the problem.

While working through a project, students may fail to use the knowledge and skills to which they have been exposed in a current or previous project. These failures provide the instructor with an opportunity to reinforce and underscore the value of prior learning. For example, one of the leaders of the *Write Right!* project chose to run the project and the meeting without using the method that had been introduced in the *Meeting Management* project. His team floundered for more than an hour and became increasingly frustrated. Sensing the growing frustration, I made the following comment: "The team isn't using the Interaction Method. It isn't clear to me why. Would you mind talking about your reasons?" The leader asked for a break; when he returned, the team proceeded to use the Interaction Method to conduct the meeting. For the remainder of the session, productivity increased and frustration decreased. During the debriefing, students talked about how valuable it had been to witness firsthand how the group functioned when it used and didn't use the Interaction Method. As a result of this experience, students increased their understanding of this particular method and became sold on its merits.

When students attempt to apply knowledge that is relevant to their problem, the instructor may discover that they apply the knowledge inappropriately. My sense is that professors vastly underestimate the prevalence and seriousness of this problem; I know that I did. By observing how students use the knowledge in dealing with a problem, instructors learn whether students understand the concepts and can translate them into action. If students misunderstand or misapply the material, the instructor can use the occasion to clarify the concept or to model its appropriate application.

Professors in a PBL instructional environment can also expect that the solution to the problem will become an issue. Lacking experience and self-confidence, students understandably want to know what constitutes a "good" or "bad" decision to the problems they are facing. I have used several different approaches to dealing with this particular issue; they seem to work. When students ask if their solution is a good one, I often respond by saying,

> In the real world, one discovers whether a decision is correct by taking action and seeing what happens. You can increase the chances of making the right decision by taking account of the crucial information, by attempting to anticipate what might go wrong, and by taking appropriate preventive or contingency actions. But, in the final analysis, you will never know with absolute certainty whether a decision works until you implement it. Being able to make decisions under these conditions comes with the territory.

Recognizing that I might judge the students' solution in terms of my own preferred course of action, I consciously avoid deciding how I would deal with the problem. Moreover, I tell students in advance that I have not tried to solve the problem and why I have chosen to act in this way.

I also seek to counteract "the good-bad" syndrome by having students view a videotape of several experienced principals discussing the problem and how they would deal with it. Students are struck with how divergent the responses of veteran principals are to the problematic situations.

Summary

In this chapter I discussed the role of the instructor and highlighted some of the challenges inherent in a PBL classroom environment. The activities of instructors during a PBL project are varied. They create, select, and sequence the projects. They assign students to project teams and designate who will be the leader, facilitator, and recorder. Instructors assemble the materials and equipment needed by project participants. Once the project is under way, the instructor acts as a process observer, provides suggestions to facilitate the team when it becomes stuck, encourages students to take risks, and provides feedback. When the project is completed, the instructor provides oral and written feedback about the team's product and performance.

While implementing a PBL project, instructors may face a variety of challenges. Students may experience difficulty in treating knowledge as a tool, may fail to use the knowledge and skills that they learned in previous projects, may apply their knowledge inappropriately, or may press the instructor to disclose what constitutes a "good" or "bad" decision to the focal problem. In this chapter I described how the instructor may deal with each of these challenges if they arise.

PBL: What Students Learn

I n the four preceding chapters, I described the rationale behind problem-based learning, how students may be introduced to a PBL environment, how PBL operates within the classroom, and what the role of the instructor is. My discussion now turns to what students learn through participating in the PBL projects that form the core of this instructional approach.

To frame this discussion, let me review some of the basic ingredients of this instructional approach. Problem-stimulated learning emphasizes three major goals: (1) the development of administrative skills, (2) the development of problem-solving skills, and (3) the acquisition of the knowledge base that underlies administrative practice. Underlying these goals is a higher-order, overarching goal, namely, that students will retrieve and appropriately use their knowledge and skills when they become administrators.

In line with the basic tenets of PBL, students are more likely to achieve these goals if they are motivated to learn the material, are enabled to acquire the knowledge and skills in a functional context, and are provided with numerous opportunities to elaborate on what they have learned. Students are motivated to learn in a PBL environment when they are provided with enjoyable and challenging activities (those that require active responses, peer interaction, higher-order thinking skills, and the completion of a product) and when their expectation of success is maintained. The latter is achieved through the choice and sequencing of projects and by supplying pertinent resources and guiding questions.

Students acquire their knowledge and skills in a functional context that makes them aware of how the knowledge and skills can be used. This context, as I have noted, contains problems they are apt to face as future administrators. Students are required to work as members of a project team to solve these problems. These projects offer students the chance to serve as team leader and, thereby, narrow the gap between the work of the student and the work of an administrator.

In a PBL environment, students are given multiple opportunities to elaborate on what they have learned. During each project, students discuss the information that was highlighted in the readings, exchange views about how the knowledge and skills might be used to deal with the focal problem, use the newly acquired information to resolve the problem, critique one another's efforts to apply the knowledge, and write essays about what they have learned. In subsequent projects, students also have opportunities to use and apply what they have learned previously.

Instructors use a variety of methods to gauge what students have learned or are learning in a PBL environment. The methods I have used include the following: (1) a direct observation of the project meetings; (2) an assessment of the team's final product, performance, or both; (3) a formal knowledge review exercise; and (4) an integrative essay that each student prepares at the end of a project. This essay encourages students to formalize what they have learned during the project. The only guidance that I provide students in preparing these essays is to suggest some questions they may choose to address. These questions are as follows:

- What principles or approaches have you learned in working with this problem that will help as you work on future problems with similar characteristics?

- What new information did you acquire that changed your knowledge and understanding of this problem?

- Is it possible for you to construct an outline, model, or generalization about the processes involved in dealing with this problem?

- What questions have been raised in working with this problem that suggest the need for further study? (If the knowledge can be acquired easily, you should do so; otherwise, note the need to pursue this information at a later time and suggest a possible study plan.)

- What have you learned about project leadership, meeting management, written communication, problem solving, and the work of the principal that might be of use to you in the future?

- What did you learn about yourself, your ability as a leader, and your participation in a management team as you worked on this project?

- What did you learn in a previous project that proved helpful in this one or needed to be revised in light of what happened during this project?

When discussing what students have learned, I will limit my discussion in two ways. First, I will confine my discussion to what they have learned about administrative skills. More specifically, I will discuss those skills that were emphasized in some of the problem-stimulated projects described in chapter 2—skills in project leadership, meeting management, memo writing, and oral presentations. Second, I will base this discussion primarily on the integrative essays prepared by students at the end of each project. Through these essays, we can gain insight into what students are learning, their emotional reactions to the learning environment, the value they place on their newly acquired knowledge and skills, and the future uses, if any, to which their knowledge might be put.

Project Leadership

The core unit of instruction in a PBL environment is a project. One of the students on each project team serves as team leader. We encourage students to use this role as a vehicle for learning about leadership and suggest a number of ways in which they might do this. We point out that the team leader role offers students the chance to:

- experiment with different leadership styles

- test theories of leadership in the crucible of practice

- create their own standards for judging their effectiveness as a leader

- obtain feedback about their leadership effectiveness from peers

- discover how they react to success and disappointment

- identify personal shortcomings that stand in the way of their becoming effective leaders

To obtain an idea of how and what students learn about leadership in the team leader role, let us examine the integrative essays of three students. A brief commentary follows each essay.

After reading this chapter, one of the students in the Prospective Principals' Program wrote:

These essays give a good sense of what students say and feel about their performance on specific projects. They are intentionally deeply reflective and thoughtful, and so do not convey the *enthusiasm* people feel about this program and the PBL method. I feel the love for the program and the method doesn't come across as strongly as it might. The affective outcomes of the process are not emphasized—the amazing camaraderie, the sensitivity to others, the change of intolerance to tolerance to acceptance to appreciation of different viewpoints—all these are important in the operational goal of the program, and in developing a new breed of administrator who won't settle for the isolation so characteristic of the principalship. Candace Simpson, 1991 graduating class.

Essay Number 1

"You're going to be the leader for the next project." My initial thoughts were "I can do that; I can run a meeting." But I was less sure about successfully managing a project. This experience would be an opportunity to refine my meeting management techniques, experiment with leadership styles, and tackle project management.

DECISIONS

At the beginning of the experience I made three conscious decisions about my leadership style and objectives.

Use a participative leadership style. I really prefer the autocratic style. Reflecting on past experiences and leadership training, however, I decided this would not work. I made a conscious commitment to try a different style, one using decision-making through consensus and majority rule rather than decree.

Finish within the project time-frame. I wanted to avoid overlap with the next project. I also felt the time limit was reasonable. In my judgment, the project could be completed in three meetings with proper planning and execution. Time constraints and inflexible deadlines are a reality in the practical workaday world. I wanted to see if we could meet such a challenge.

Achieve group satisfaction with the product and the process. I knew my group could finish on time, one way or another. "Come Hell or high water!," I remember saying. However, I did not want to achieve the time objective at the expense of interpersonal relationships.

FEEDBACK

The decisions I made at the beginning of the project were the parameters by which I measured my success and effectiveness as a leader. I wanted feedback from the group to validate my own evaluations and perceptions. Did I actually use participative leadership? Did I lead the group to an on-time finish without sacrificing satisfaction with the process or product? I also wanted feedback on my strengths and areas for improvement. A critique sheet distributed at the end of the project provided this feedback (the feedback questions appear at the end of this essay). I also wanted feedback on whether the group met its objectives. This was obtained verbally at the end of the last group meeting.

The feedback that I received verbally and from the critique sheets was very positive and encouraging. It substantiated my own evaluation of my performance as group leader. According to the team members, I was organized, well prepared, and task-oriented. They thought I provided structure and control yet was open to group ideas. I ensured equal participation and led the group to decisions made by consensus or majority rule. These were my strengths identified by the group. All members were satisfied with the process and the product. They enjoyed the group and would want to be in a group I was leading. Verbal feedback indicated that they felt we accomplished our established objectives.

LESSONS LEARNED

What did I learn from the feedback and the experience? I learned that participative leadership can actually produce timely and efficient results; and I could use this style effectively. At the beginning of the project, I had little confidence in participative leadership. I doubted that a group could efficiently produce a product in a timely manner using consensus. This influenced my preference for individual memos.

The rest of the group, however, thought differently. Letting majority rule, we agreed to produce a group memo. Using a mixture of consensus and majority rule, the group produced a team memo within the time established and to the satisfaction of all members. My views on participative leadership subsequently changed. Nevertheless, I still believe there is a time and place for persuasion and authoritative rule.

The value of group work was reinforced through this experience. Working as a group provided opportunity to capitalize on multiple strengths and viewpoints. Reflecting back, I think the decisions made by the group were better overall than individual decisions. The group memo was better, in my opinion, than my own or any other individual memo. The final plan of action determined by the group was also better than my plan alone.

I gained a new perspective on the role of the leader. Midway through the project I realized I was feeling very stressed about the project. I felt I must determine the "right" answer and then sell it to the group. Reflecting on this, I concluded that wasn't *my* responsibility as the leader. Problem-solving was the *group's* responsibility. Reflecting further on past leadership experiences, I surmised that this misplaced sense of responsibility might account for my dissatisfaction with other group experiences. If I didn't want to revert to autocracy, my role was to facilitate, clarify, and guide the process. As a very wise professor once said: "The leader's job is to lead the *group* where *they* want to go, and help them decide where that is if they don't know."

The most important thing I learned, however, is that I am a good leader and project manager already! Realizing this, I will continue what I already do well—organize, plan, attend to details, prepare, remain task-oriented, keep to time schedules. I can improve, though, by continuing the participative style I tried in this experience—an agenda open to revision by the group, decision-making through a mixture of consensus and majority-rule, equal participation of group members, meeting closure with a review of accomplishments, and followup actions.

Another change would be something I did not do well in this experience or previous leadership experiences—active listening. At times I caught myself not listening but planning my response. In the future I will make a conscious decision and effort to listen actively. Lastly, I would act on the only suggestion for improvement given by one of my group: "Relax, have more confidence in yourself and in the group!"

CONCLUSIONS

This was a very valuable and satisfying experience. I met my objectives, expanded my leadership skills, and renewed my confidence. I needed to feel successful and effective, and I DID!

Feedback on Group Leader (Critique Sheet)

Please provide a constructive critique of my leadership. Be honest and as specific as possible.

1. How well did I facilitate the group process throughout the project?
2. Did I ensure that all members participated equally and had an opportunity to express their views/opinions?
3. Was responsibility delegated appropriately?
4. Do you think I was too structured or excessively controlled the group?
5. Did you enjoy the group? If I were the leader of some other group you were assigned to, would you want to be in the group? Why or why not?
6. Were you satisfied with the group process and product? If not, with what specifically were you dissatisfied?
7. What did I do particularly well as the leader? What suggestions do you have for improvement?
8. Comments:

Commentary

This student approached her leadership role with several objectives in mind. She indicated her intention to experiment with a participative leadership style, a style that was being emphasized in the PBL curriculum. This style, as she acknowledges in her essay, was not her preferred one; moreover, she harbored some serious reservations about the effectiveness of this leadership style.

The standards she established for judging her leadership effectiveness were consistent with the ones that had been underscored in the curriculum, namely, accomplishing the project objectives within the prescribed time limits without sacrificing team member satisfaction with the process. Finally, she sought feedback from team members about how she had performed her role and suggestions for improvement. By soliciting feedback, she again was behaving consistently with what was being modeled and advocated in the curriculum.

What did she learn in her role as project leader? From the vantage point of the program, she changed her views about participative leadership in the desired direction. She discovered that she could use this leadership style effectively and expressed the intention to use it in the future. Although the feedback she received from team members was quite supportive and revealed no apparent weaknesses, she recognized that she tended not to engage in active listening and vowed to work on this issue in the future. Her self-critical stance is a healthy one and mirrors what we strive to model in the program.

This student's essay also reveals how she was conceptualizing and reacting to the instructional environment. She clearly saw the activities as challenging, emotionally engaging, and satisfying. At the same time she viewed what she was doing from the perspective of a leader, invested considerable thought and effort into enacting this role, and valued what she had learned in the process. Her responses were consistent with expectations inherent in the rationale underlying the use of PBL in preparing administrators.

Essay Number 2

In the past few years I have read many books and articles on leadership, and I have formally studied leadership in two courses here at Stanford. Nevertheless, my recent experience as a group leader has perhaps taught me more than all of the reading and study combined. While reading and study may provide general ideas about effective leadership and give one a knowledge base from which to operate, it is in actual practice—with specific issues, contexts, and personalities—that one may discover more about leadership, about one's particular leadership style, and about ways one can make that style more effective and more satisfying. Furthermore, actual practice transforms the reading and study into meaningful information, so that theory and practice begin to inform each other.

As leader of one of the two project teams, I resolved to put into practice some of the ideas I had read about or studied recently. Unfortunately, as I discovered, the transition from theory to practice is not as smooth as I had expected—a lesson I've learned before but have never fully accepted. When you're interacting with specific individuals—each of whom has expectations for a leader and "ways of seeing" leadership—the use of general theoretical principles may be highly ineffective. Above all else, perhaps, I learned that leaders should try to understand the needs, desires, and expectations of group members from the very start and also communicate clearly to them their own needs, desires, and expectations.

I wanted everyone in the group to lead in some fashion. Because of that theoretical bias, I announced at the start that I believed in shared leadership and consensus decision-making. Although everyone seemed to accept that position, they had little opportunity to say what they expected of me or of the way the group should function. (I made this a specific agenda item but never really developed it.) In a sense, then, I was autocratically stating that I wanted shared leadership, a position that may have undermined what I hoped would happen. The mere hope of embodying theory in practice seems shortsighted and simplistic; leadership must be well planned and must adapt theory to specific situations and personalities.

In short, I simply announced that I wanted to lead with an informal style that would emphasize consensus, mutual participation, sharing, nurturing, and cooperation. Members of the group agreed that such a stance was appropriate, though I think all of us wondered how that would facilitate the completion of the task at hand and in what manner each would lead. I also noted, however, that I might tend in actual practice to espouse consensus but act in an authoritative way (had I already?), that I might not listen to others as carefully as I should, and that I might overdo my responsibilities because I perceived that a leader should do more than others. Those, I said, were concerns that I wanted the group to check me on and to evaluate.

Given this stance, our first meeting was inevitably a rather random session in which we discussed how we should proceed. Despite my fairly clear agenda and my opening remarks about how I perceived my role and what I thought should underlie our group (fairness, equal responsibility, satisfaction and growth for all, completion of task by the deadline), the meeting proceeded without any clear structure or order. Each group member participated and seemed to enjoy the meeting, and everyone left with a clear sense of what he or she should accomplish by the next meeting. Nevertheless, I came out of the meeting feeling quite anxious and defeated, as though I hadn't provided enough structure and as though I hadn't led a meeting that in any way resembled the kinds of meetings discussed in our readings. Indeed, when I asked the group how they thought the meeting had gone, they offered very few substantial remarks, and I took that as a sign that I hadn't done an adequate job of leading.

Still, we had had a good discussion of the case and had begun to think about the issues and how we would approach them. Thanks to A, we began to focus on short-term versus long-term objectives; thanks to B, we began to focus on ethical issues; and thanks to C, we came out of the meeting with a resolve that each of us would prepare a way of approaching the case and outline what we believed was the main idea in the case by the time we met again. My own contribution was to suggest some of the social, community issues in the case—something we eventually incorporated into our long-term alternatives.

The next day I distributed copies of notes about our meeting and a list of questions I had been considering. The notes probably helped keep us focused. The questions, however, clearly reflected my own thinking about the case and probably shouldn't have been inflicted upon the group at this point. Those questions, as well as a piece I wrote up by way of preparing for the next meeting, describe my own mind-set and my strong desire at that time to see the case solely in terms of community social problems.

When we met again the next Tuesday, I outlined an agenda on the blackboard and asked if anyone wanted to add agenda items or change the sequence of my agenda. (That was the procedure used as well in the next two meetings.) A few items were added. Thus, I was still eager to pursue the idea of shared leadership with the group, though I wanted desperately to make sure we remained focused and on task. Fortunately, C and D, both of whom have considerable knowledge of public school systems, "took the ball" and ran with it during this meeting, though all five members certainly contributed to our discussion. D was particularly helpful in outlining the discussion points on the board and then in working up a flowchart for our eventual memo. In fact, all members seemed to assume some leadership from this point on, and it looked as though the group was adopting a successful scheme of shared leadership.

Yet I felt uneasy again after that second meeting. C and D obviously had knowledge that I didn't, and they expressed that knowledge in a way that clearly helped the group and its progress toward the completion of the memo. For much of the meeting I listened to their excellent remarks and was delighted that we seemed to be accomplishing a great deal. At the same time, however, I felt as though I should have been doing more to lead, that others were doing the leading that I should have been doing. (Perhaps I was equating knowledge with power, and power with leadership.) No doubt my ego was getting in the way of my perception of things. We were, after all, doing exactly what I had hoped we would do, though now it seemed to me that I had had very little to do with the remarkable way in which theory (shared leadership) and practice were coinciding.

I remembered reading somewhere that the best leaders don't seem to be leading at all, and I appeased myself by believing that that was what had happened here; but I also had the nagging feeling that the group might have been equally successful without me. In any case, I was struggling with leadership issues—shared leadership versus a structured, centered leadership; leadership as listening versus leadership as the assertion of authority; an evolving group structure versus an ordered, set group structure, etc.—and I was learning a great deal from that struggle about myself, my interaction in groups, and my understanding of the relationship between theory and practice.

I would note, too, that I learned much from the content of the second meeting. It was difficult for me, for example, to let go of a favorite notion—the community social issue. While other members of the group had exciting ideas in their own right, I pressed my own and perhaps didn't help them develop theirs as I might have. I learned, I think, that I must let go or modify my own point of view, no matter how valid it seems, and listen to the perspectives of others in the group. Moreover, I learned a little more about how and why others might have objections to my point of view, why they might not see it in the same way I do, and why their alternative perspectives might be more valid than my point of view. I would also note that I learned something about how what may seem to be most right in a general sense may not be best or right in specific circumstances. Situational leadership, adaptability, and flexibility—those may be extremely important to any leader.

Two other notes here: (1) I became quite attached to the "shared governance" notion of evaluation used in Salt Lake City, and I probably mistakenly tried to impose this notion upon the issues of our case. In some sense, I would suggest, my desire to see our group exercise shared leadership parallels my fondness for the "shared governance" in Salt Lake City. Those may both be excellent ways of proceeding, of course, but I recognize that I must be careful not to let idealism inform every situation, especially when some situations may call for very different kinds of leadership or governance. I'm suggesting, thus, that I must be careful not to be politically naive. (2) I think I overprepared my thoughts for this meeting and, as a result, became overly attached to them. Leaders, it seems clear, must not confuse the significance of particular ideas with the amount of time or energy invested in them.

Our third meeting went very well, I thought, with all five members actively contributing to the discussion, and I came away feeling good about our progress and our resolve to complete the memo at the next meeting, to be held at D's house. Each member helped generate pros and cons for our five alternatives, and I sensed that all were satisfied with the progress we were making and confident that we could complete our task in one further meeting. Remarkably enough, we were all sharing the responsibility for leading the group.

The long final meeting once again saw everyone contributing. D did an outstanding job on the computer, A presented her very clear alternative, C consistently offered good suggestions on almost everything, B provided an extraordinarily sensible evaluation plan, and I felt guilty for having to leave early to pick up my wife. The group completed the thorough and well-constructed memo without me, a fact that makes me a little uneasy about the role I was supposed to have played but that showed that this was indeed a group led by all members.

Altogether, then, I feel very good about the way this group worked together and about the lessons I learned along the way. I still have some anxiety over the tension between shared leadership, which I like to espouse, and a more structured, centered leadership, to which I've been socialized for most of my life. But I'm learning how to cope with that anxiety and, I hope, how to transform it into flexibility and situational leadership. Most importantly, I think I've learned a little more about how to listen, how to give up or modify my positions, and how leadership means much more than making my presence felt or heard.

Commentary

In this extended essay, the student discusses how he elected to use the project leader role to advance his understanding of leadership. During his study of leadership in other courses, he became enamored with shared leadership. His role as team leader provided him with an opportunity to put his pet notion of leadership into practice. Secondarily, he wanted feedback from his team about whether his leadership practices were consistent with the tenets of shared leadership, whether he was an attentive listener, and whether he took on more responsibilities than he should. Since we underscore that PBL provides a relatively risk-free laboratory for testing theory in practice and securing feedback about one's leadership practices, his intentions were certainly appropriate.

During the project, he learned something that simply is not possible in a conventional instructional environment. Although the team finished its product on time, team members were satisfied with the process, and they shared the leadership responsibilities, he did not find the leadership style personally satisfying. He desired to have his presence as a leader felt and heard; when he sensed that it was not, he experienced considerable tension and anxiety. Although he claims that the experience taught him "how leadership means much more than making my presence felt or heard," it is also clear that he has not resolved the tension he feels between shared and centralized forms of leadership. A style of shared leadership may simply be incompatible with this student's personality, a possibility that he seems unwilling to entertain at this time.

In this student's essay, we see how his prior knowledge about leadership has been activated in the PBL environment and been put to a test in the crucible of practice. His words capture an important feature of PBL:

> While reading and study may provide general ideas about effective leadership and give one a knowledge base from which to operate, it is in actual practice—with specific issues, contexts, and personalities—that one may discover more about leadership, about

one's particular leadership style, and about ways one can make that style more effective and more satisfying. Furthermore, actual practice transforms the reading and study into meaningful information, so that theory and practice begin to inform each other.

As we anticipated given the rationale underlying PBL, this student seems to be highly motivated, to consider the activities challenging, and to have found the experience extremely valuable, though discomforting at times.

Essay Number 3

Why was this such an unsatisfying experience?

It felt like a failure—individual and collective; and I feel responsible for not helping the group to resolve our difficulties with the assignment....

Why wasn't I able to help the group do this?

1. The "mess" was confusing to me. There were so many facets to the problem, particularly those drawing on knowledge of or experience with the district office or a districtwide perspective, that I repeatedly lost sight of the thrust of our discussion as we circled back into the problem. An example of this occurred in the first session when we began clumping issues rather than continuing to separate them. I directed this because the process we were in was making the situation more confusing rather than more clear. My strategy was counterproductive because it led us away from the simpler, smaller problems. We should have persisted with "separation techniques."

2. I did not ask for help. I should have asked A— how they were able to come up with a solution so neatly. We had talked beforehand, and I did not initiate the conversation that might have helped me and the group discover a new approach. I should have asked Ed when the task became overwhelming. This is too typical of my behavior. Despite enjoying work with groups, I don't easily move beyond self-imposed restrictions to ask for help from experts outside the "supposed" parameters. By limiting myself in this way to a rigid set of self-imposed rules of what I am supposed to do, I lose opportunities to find new solutions....

As to pressure and priorities, I give too much authority to external authorities—bosses, assignments, etc.—and so lose sight of people priorities outside of the job. To be specific, during this experience I sacrificed my family relationships at a critical time (for them). This was irresponsible. It would have been smarter to sacrifice the assignment, and to find a way to do this without betraying the group. This was not a unique experience. I have to learn how to put the job in better perspective with the rest of my life and with the world context. A simulation is pretty small in the whole scheme of things. Furthermore, by making the assignment and my responsibility for it too big a deal in my own mind, I also limited my creativity in trying to help the group be more creative and less stressed.

I found the board feedback accurate. Both products were weak:

1. The memo *was* confusing and cluttered. I settled for the result when time ran out. I gave up, and we turned in what we did.

2. The meeting was unsatisfying, and not just because they sent us back for a revision. I *did* set the meeting with the Board off to a bad start by including them in the previous decision rather than accepting responsibility myself for a previous poor decision. They became testy in response, and their feedback at the end was accurate. I *didn't* listen well. My unresolved distaste for the assignment and my impatience with their "interruptions" to our presentation were uncreative. Rather than flowing with the experience, I resisted it and antagonized them. Not very smart. I didn't anticipate that they would direct the flow of the session from the beginning. I did step out of the simulation to comment about the "givens" rather than being creative on the spot.

So despite the fact that I still have strong reservations about the framing of the initial task, the project has important lessons for me to ponder and issues to resolve. That is of value, and for that I am grateful. I find it difficult to fail, but no one died, and if I can learn about making mistakes and carrying on creatively despite them, particularly in not letting initial difficulties get me down, that will be progress.

Commentary

During this project the leader, by his own admission, tasted disappointment and feelings of failure, sentiments that virtually all leaders experience at one time or another in their career. Nothing seemed to work. The team's efforts to solve the "messy" problem floundered and proved frustrating throughout the project. Despite working "overtime," the group created a "confusing and cluttered" memo about what should be done to resolve the problem. Its presentation to the board of education was also dissatisfying; the board raised numerous objections to the team's proposal and declined to approve it in its current form. As is evident in the student's essay, he assumed responsibility for what transpired and struggled to transform this unpleasant experience into a learning opportunity.

The most valuable lesson that he learned is captured in this sentence: "I have to learn how to put the job in better perspective with the rest of my life and with the world context." This experience underscored for him his tendency to take work too seriously and to behave ineffectively whenever things weren't going well. For the next two years, he consciously strove to change his perspective on life. As graduation neared, he told me, "That experience, painful as it was at the time, has added ten years to my life. I now have a much better sense of what's important and what isn't. Even the important things don't bother me the way they used to."

Even though we attempt to program students for success, the projects are sufficiently challenging that students generally encounter failure at least once in the process of completing the program. These occasions become opportunities for students to learn how to manage disappointment. Admittedly, the learning that occurs rarely reaches the level attained by the student who prepared this essay.

Meeting Management

The meeting management project aims to teach students how to manage meetings using the interaction method. They read about this method in a book titled *How to Make Meetings Work*. During the life of the project, students are expected to use this method while working on the desert survival problem and preparing their written analysis of the group's process as it worked on the problem. The essay that follows reveals what one student learned during this project and what her reactions were to her initial encounter with PBL.

Essay Number 4

W, newly appointed principal at M Jr. High, called a staff meeting to select recipients of graduation awards. Every year the staff weathers an emotionally charged meeting during which winners for several community and departmental awards are chosen. Perhaps because W had never participated in the awards meeting, she asked our vice-principal to facilitate and be recorder of the meeting.

O, who is our math department chairman as well, had barely convened the meeting when several problems arose; some wished to balance awards by sex, others wanted no restrictions placed on selection. A few staff members felt the awards should be given to a variety of deserving students, yet others felt an award should be given to the most deserving student regardless of other recognition. People also argued about which awards should be selected first, general or departmental. Throughout all this disagreement, O gave his input to the content of the discussion and then pressed the group to make a decision so we could leave by 4:30 p.m. The two-hour meeting resulted in much shouting. Several people left before adjournment, and only a few awards were confirmed.

I believe the meeting was a very frustrating and unpleasant experience for all in attendance. When I left that meeting, I didn't know what had caused the problem. I knew I felt badly about the content of the decisions and disappointed in many of my colleagues. I wasn't sure which part of the task still needed to be accomplished or when we might meet again to finish designating the awards. I deeply cared about acknowledging students' achievement, but if it was necessary to subject myself to that type of meeting, maybe I would make up some excuse to avoid a followup session.

After reading *How to Make Meetings Work* and participating in the practicum exercise, I have a clear understanding of the causes of the failure of the awards selection meeting. Our staff had failed to make a distinction between process and content, objectives weren't clearly stated, roles weren't clearly defined and adhered to, and a variety of unspoken personal expectations led to communication problems and personality conflicts. In the years to come, the staff will continue to recognize deserving students with awards at graduation. In order to ensure a more satisfying, productive experience for the staff, I would make the following recommendations:...[9 in all based on the principles of the Interaction Method].

After working with my teammates on the survival exercise, I am acutely aware of the value of using the interaction method to ensure successful meeting management. The basic principles of role definition, separation of process and content, and the step-by-step procedure for problem solving as described in the book are valuable tools for ensuring productive group work. During the survival exercise, I enjoyed participating in the problem solving because I felt part of a hard working team committed to meeting the product objectives as well as the learning objectives. The group product exceeded that which most of us would have produced on our own. I left the meetings energized, yet exhausted. We had worked hard and accomplished a great deal.

It is my hope that the M Junior High School staff will experience the same sense of accomplishment as they tackle the variety of problems facing educators today. There is no question that a well-run staff meeting should produce similar results.

Commentary

This student's essay seems to follow the script that we had in mind when we designed the project. In line with our hoped-for outcomes, she views her newly acquired knowledge as a tool. In her essay she uses the concepts from the interaction method to diagnose why a staff meeting she had attended was so frustrating and unproductive. Moreover, she uses the concepts to prescribe how a future staff meeting on the same issue might be structured to ensure a more satisfying, productive experience. This essay has stimulated her to elaborate on her knowledge and to consider how it might be used to her advantage in real-life settings.

Equally important from our vantage point, she, according to our expectations, was highly motivated to learn the material. In the process of using it, she and others expended considerable effort on the learning tasks and enjoyed participating in the planned activities. By the time the project was completed, she had experienced success (in her words, "sense of accomplishment") and had become sold on the value of using the method to run successful meetings. We attribute her reactions in large part to the design of the problem-based learning project that conformed to the rationale summarized at the beginning of this chapter.

Memo Writing

The *Write Right!* project teaches students about memo writing. Specifically, students are expected to learn a reader-centered approach to written communication and a system for editing and revising their memos. During this project, students read about these two approaches, study a "messy" problem that has surfaced in the school where they are principal, prepare a memo to the superintendent about the situation, and edit one another's memos prior to submitting the final version to the superintendent.

Besides teaching students memo-writing skills, this project provides students with an opportunity to use the problem-solving, project-management, and meeting-management skills they have acquired in previous projects. In this way, the project activates their prior knowledge and provides them with another chance to elaborate on this knowledge. The integrative essay that follows reflects what one of the students reports she learned during the *Write Right!* project.

Essay Number 5

The principles of concise, persuasive writing will serve me throughout my career. As a principal, I will need to communicate with various audiences in writing. The ability to do so briefly and effectively will enhance my effectiveness. *The principle of writing with the reader in mind, or getting inside the mind of the reader, is very powerful.* I have seen many memos written that were too full of jargon, too wordy, or too technical to reach their intended audiences. I frequently need to write letters, notes, or bulletins to parents regarding school events. I often take them to my aides and ask them to let me know if they are too complicated. For parents who may be speakers of other languages or who are not familiar with school talk, this skill is essential. *The principle of frontloading is another very powerful tool.* We are given so much written material in schools that we must find ways to get and give the maximum amount of information in the minimum amount of time. *The third principle I learned was avoiding the lard.* As a wordy writer, this will be very helpful to me. I have had experience before with group editing of my own writing, and I am always surprised at how much simplification improves my style. However, none of these skills is easy to learn. I will need much more practice to be able to use them effectively. I think that I will ask myself these questions from now on when I write a memo:

Did I say what the reader needs to hear in a way that he/she can most effectively hear it?

Did I put the most important words and thoughts first?

Did I use words frugally and eliminate unnecessary phrases?

Commentary

In this brief essay the student reveals that she has learned three principles for writing memos. She derived these principles from the reading materials that were included with the *Write Right!* project. Moreover, she translated the three principles into three questions that she will bear in mind as she prepares future memos. Both her principles and her questions are consistent with the project's two major learning objectives.

In the essay she implies that she found the material meaningful and valuable when she stated that these principles will serve her throughout her career. She also acknowledges that she will need much more practice to use these principles effectively. This belief is consistent with our view and drives our decision to create memo-writing opportunities for students in subsequent projects.

Her essay is silent on whether she learned the formatting techniques that were emphasized in the project. These techniques included such matters as using headings and subheadings, writing short paragraphs, using "block left" formatting, using stars or bullets to highlight important points or recommendations, and exploiting the white space on each page. Although she used these techniques in preparing her memo to the superintendent, she did not use any of these techniques when preparing her essay, either because she failed to recognize that they were useful in this context or because she does not consider them particularly worthwhile. Since she did not underscore the value of these techniques in her essay, the second possibility is certainly a reasonable one and provides the instructor with an opportunity to explore this issue with the student.

Oral Communication

In *Present Your Case!* students learn how to make several different types of oral presentations. The project centers around a curriculum problem facing a high school principal, namely, how to incorporate a controversial topic, AIDS, into the high school curriculum. Members of the project team form the membership of the high school curriculum committee and are empowered to decide which role-groups will be represented on the committee.

The project culminates in an oral presentation to the local board of education (roles played by individuals who are current or former board members in real life) by the members of the curriculum committee. Each team member is required to participate in this board presentation. In addition, the team is expected to provide board members with a written report that the committee wants read prior to the meeting. By structuring the project in this way, we create an opportunity for students to acquire new knowledge while using the skills from previous projects, namely, skills in project and meeting management, problem-solving, and written communication. In the following essay, one of the students discusses what he learned from participating in this project.

Essay Number 6

During the second session of this project, I caught myself advocating for a board-appointed representative to fill the slot on the presenting committee. I, a longtime advocate of liberal causes, had just supported excluding a student from the presenting panel. Why?!? I would have never taken this seemingly "conservative" position in the past.

I now realize that I took this position because my view of school administration had begun to change. I based my response to the issue of finalizing the presenting panel on a few important principles of presentation. These principles stress wise planning and decision-making. Below, I will examine the presentation principles that I consider important and explore how these may help me in the future.

First, I learned in this project that there are many ways to organize a presentation. There are presentation formats that serve merely to organize information to be passed on to a group. There are also more sophisticated formats like Monroe's Motivator that allow presenters to organize information in a way that motivates an audience and increases the persuasive power of a presentation. These formats are very helpful in planning presentations. They will be especially helpful to me in planning presentations I make to fellow teachers on curriculum innovations. They will also be helpful in my future work in school administration, e.g., board presentations.

Second, I learned about a series of valuable techniques on analyzing an audience. Some of these techniques range from anticipating questions members of an audience may raise to formulating counterarguments to possible objections from an audience. I found these techniques especially useful in preparing for our presentation to the mock board. Our group's work in this area really paid off. We considered thoroughly the possible objections from the board and analyzed extensively each board member's stance on the issue. I plan to use these techniques in my future work, especially in dealing with the board and other political bodies.

Third, I value greatly the suggestions made in the readings about ways to connect with an audience. This approach might be done on individual members of an audience if it is a small group. For example, if there is a particular board member with a predictable political stance, it will be useful to explore ways in which the presenters might find common ground with this board member.

Having had these experiences, I now realize that presenting involves planning about the topic as well as planning aimed at anticipating specific reactions from an audience. This is a new way of thinking for me. In the past I would have considered this process "playing politics." In certain ways it is "playing politics," but it is also considering a topic thoroughly. Undertaking this process means considering the alternative view points. It involves getting into other people's shoes. This process is a *responsible* way of doing business because it allows you to consider all aspects of an issue.

Commentary

In this student's essay, he discusses what he learned from the *Present Your Case!* project and how he intends to use these ideas in the future. According to him, he learned different ways to organize a presentation, techniques for analyzing an audience, and ways to connect with an audience. Since each of these ideas was stressed in the project, his reported learning corresponds to our intentions. His account clearly underscores that he found the ideas valuable and worth using in other settings. His proposed uses are sensible and appropriate.

Perhaps the most intriguing part of this student's essay is his revelations about how his perspective is changing. By his own admission, he is beginning to adopt an administrator's perspective, one that had been alien to him in the past but now seems both responsible and functional. In part, this shift is occurring because of our conscious effort to create a learning environment in which the work of the student corresponds more closely to the work of an administrator. The task environment is having a socializing effect on this student and assisting him in making the transition to the role of an administrator.

Summary

In this chapter I have discussed what students learn in a problem-stimulated learning environment. My discussion is limited in several respects. It focuses primarily on only one of the curriculum's major goals, namely, the development of administrative skills (most notably skills in project and meeting management, memo writing, and oral presentations). The discussion is based on the integrative essays students prepare at the end of each project. Through the discussion, I have endeavored to illustrate what students report learning about these skills, how students react to the instructional environment, and how their learning and reactions relate to the rationale and design of a PBL curriculum.

Since the discussion is admittedly limited and highly selective, a few additional comments are in order. The essays that have been included in this chapter fall into the upper quartile as far as quality is concerned. Some students produce essays that are not nearly as thoughtful or informative. In such cases, I base my judgments about what students have learned on other sources—observations of these students during the life of a project and reviews of their final products and performance.

Although the essays I chose to present are not representative in terms of quality, they are representative in another sense. Most students in a PBL environment react as did the students who wrote these essays. They generally are highly motivated, enjoy what they are doing, recognize the value of what they are learning, think about how they will use their newly acquired knowledge and skills as future administrators, and experience a sense of accomplishment upon completion of a project.

Implementing Problem-Based Learning in a Higher Education Context

U p to this point, I have discussed a variety of topics related to problem-based learning. By now readers should have an understanding of what problem-based learning is and the rationale behind it. Moreover, they should possess insight into how PBL may be incorporated into a program for preparing educational administrators. Finally, readers should have some idea of what students may learn through this instructional approach.

On the assumption that this discussion has stimulated an interest in experimenting with problem-based learning, readers probably are asking the following question: How do we proceed to implement this approach? More specifically, what are the barriers to be surmounted and how might these obstacles be overcome? This chapter seeks to illuminate these important issues.

Potential Barriers

Problem-based learning is an innovation; like most innovations, its implementation is hardly straightforward. Numerous obstacles await those who decide to try this approach. Although these barriers to adoption undoubtedly will vary from one institution to another, some are quite predictable and are likely to be present in nearly every institution. Based on what we have read and experienced ourselves, the most frequently occurring barriers relate to the institutional reward system, the scarcity of resources, and the pre-existing attitudes and expertise of faculty.

Lack of Extrinsic Rewards

Organizations are giant Skinner-boxes dispensing rewards for some behaviors and punishment for others. Higher education organizations differentially value teaching, research, publication, service, and fundraising. Despite public declarations to the contrary, professors recognize that certain behaviors, namely, research, publication, and fundraising, are far more likely to be rewarded than teaching. (Have professors ever considered the possibility that they might secure external funding to buy release time from research and publication? Certainly not; the possibility is unthinkable.)

As long as this reward system prevails, most professors understandably will seek to maximize their rewards by engaging in those behaviors that their institution weights most heavily when determining salary increases and promotions. Since PBL is an instructional innovation, the institution is unlikely to provide extrinsic rewards that act as incentives for professors to use this approach. Instead, the reward system may actually create disincentives.

Scarcities of Time and Money

Two types of resources may also serve as barriers to implementing PBL. The first of these is time, a scarce resource in nearly every organization. PBL makes at least two major demands on professors that exceed those inherent in conventional instruction. Based on our experience with PBL, we recognize that creating instructional materials consumes a great deal of time. Each PBL project requires from 120 to 160 hours to construct, field-test, and revise. As one becomes familiar with the process, the time consumed moves closer to the lower estimate than the higher one.

PBL also may involve spending more contact hours with students. We have found it difficult to manage more than three groups (five to seven students each) simultaneously. To maximize the outcomes from this kind of approach, we have deemed it advisable to limit the number of students being taught at one time by dividing a PBL-based course into two or more sections. Consequently, the professor may double or triple the time spent with students in teaching the course. In some of the medical schools offering a dual track, professors who choose to teach in the PBL track also teach in the conventional track. Their instructional responsibilities in the PBL track represent an overload that they voluntarily accept because of their strong commitment to this approach.

A university's budget sets limits on what the organization may undertake. The more enlightened and perhaps more well-to-do universities (a vanishing breed) earmark 1 to 2 percent of increases in the budget for new initiatives. Most, however, lack the resources to implement such a policy. As a result, those who adopt PBL must compete with more established programs for the fiscal resources needed to implement the program.

To implement PBL, faculty will require release time for course planning. If instructors are hired on a temporary basis to replace faculty who are involved in planning PBL-based courses, funds must be provided for this purpose.

Additional money may also be required to purchase equipment (examples are video cameras, microphones, VCRs, electronic chalkboards, and easels), instructional materials (such as films and cases), and supplies (for example, butcher paper, marking pens, and blank videotapes). If program planners choose to use practitioners who are expert on the content of particular projects as consultants, funds will be needed to underwrite these costs as well.

Preference for Traditional Instruction

Faculty knowledge, skills, and attitudes represent a third potential barrier to implementing problem-based learning. Few faculty members are aware of what PBL is, the forms it may take, the rationale underlying it, and how it operates.

Most faculty members have been taught by the two instructional methods most commonly used in preparing educational administrators—lecture and discussion. As a result, they probably lack a number of the skills inherent in problem-based learning. Some of the major skills likely to be missing include proficiency in creating PBL projects, expertise in using the method as a mode of classroom instruction, and skills in recognizing and solving problems that may arise in the course of a problem-based learning project.

Faculty members may also harbor attitudes about instruction and learning that may prevent them from considering problem-based learning. They may be convinced that students will not actually learn what they need to know unless the instructor stands and delivers. Moreover, some professors may even regard their teaching as being synonymous with student learning. Professors with convictions like these and/or strong attachments to the ways in which they were taught will be reluctant to try an instructional approach that radically alters the role of teacher and student. Their faith in and fondness for "tried and true" instructional approaches are potentially formidable barriers to adopting and implementing PBL.

A Possible Strategy

Overcoming these barriers requires a comprehensive strategy. The one that we propose emanates from the knowledge that we have gained from the field of medical education and from our own firsthand experience with implementing PBL. Our proposed strategy consists of four major stages: (1) raising funds from external sources, (2) using PBL projects or materials that have been developed elsewhere, (3) developing one's own PBL projects, and (4) disseminating the results.

Raising Funds from External Sources

Virtually every PBL program seeks and uses external funds to initiate the program. These funds provide some measure of legitimacy for the effort and offset the one-time-only expenses associated with introducing PBL. The major expenses, as we have noted, relate to release time for faculty planning, instructional equipment, supplies, and materials. Without external funding for these startup costs, it will be extremely difficult to overcome the barriers inherent in implementing PBL.

Foundations are perhaps the single best funding source for initiating a PBL program. They are especially interested in funding programs that depart boldly from traditional practices, meet a compelling need, describe clearly and concisely how the need will be met, are reasonably priced, and are likely to be sustained after the foundation funds disappear. A problem-based learning program matches these criteria. The problem-stimulated projects referred to in this book have been supported by the Walter S. Johnson Foundation and the Danforth Foundation.

Using PBL Materials Developed Elsewhere

In light of the vast amount of time involved in creating problem-based learning projects from scratch, we deem it advisable to initiate a trial of this instructional approach with projects and materials already available. By using and/or modifying projects developed elsewhere, faculty members may substantially reduce the amount of time that they must invest in testing PBL and devote their time mainly to discovering how they and their students react to this new approach.

When PBL is introduced into medical schools, faculty members often borrow materials from schools with established PBL programs and either modify these materials consistent with their needs and purposes or use the materials intact. Whenever possible, we also have used problems or cases that were already available. The problem-based learning projects that appear in this book may be used by other institutions wishing to try this approach.

If a group of faculty decides to implement PBL on a trial basis, the following steps may be followed when using projects or materials developed elsewhere:

1. *Develop a knowledge base by reading about PBL.* Chapter 1 describes what PBL is and the rationale behind it, chapter 2 highlights how it may be introduced to students, and chapter 3 describes how PBL is used in the classroom. Those who wish to delve more deeply into the nature of PBL may read a number of the references that appear in the bibliography.

2. *Assume the role of students in a problem-based learning project.* The knowledge base acquired in step 1 will provide faculty members with some insight into the concept of PBL. Their understanding of how it operates in the classroom can be expanded by assuming the role of students and working through one or more of the PBL projects contained in Appendix B. This kind of exposure will also sensitize faculty members to what students are feeling and learning through this instructional approach. Moreover, the fac-

ulty will be able to anticipate the kinds of problems students are likely to encounter when they begin working on a project.

3. *Assume the role of instructor in a problem-based learning project.* Sections of chapters 1, 2, and especially 4 spell out what the instructor's role is in a PBL project. In chapter 4, I further highlight some of the major challenges confronting instructors and suggest how these challenges may be overcome. Undoubtedly, other problems and issues may arise that will baffle the instructor. If a regular forum is created for faculty members to discuss these concerns with one another, they are much more likely to be satisfactorily resolved.

Developing Problem-Stimulated Learning Projects

Based on the results of using PBL projects that have been developed elsewhere, instructors may decide to develop their own. In chapter 2, I list eight features of problem-based learning projects instructors may wish to take into account when designing their own. Regardless of the features they decide to include, instructors are likely to face the following issues:

1. How does one begin?

2. What problems should be used, and how should they be presented?

3. What kinds of products and product specifications should be included in a project?

4. What kinds of resources should be included in a project?

5. How important is it to field-test a PBL project?

In the remainder of this section, I will discuss these five issues and what I have learned about them. Perhaps this discussion will assist others in grappling with these same issues.

Issue 1: How does one begin?

When I began developing problem-stimulated learning projects, I started in familiar territory with user-friendly issues. These were issues in which I had already acquired a theoretical, research, and practical background—selection, supervision, evaluation, and group process. Only after I had created a number of problem-based learning projects on these familiar issues did I begin to explore unfamiliar territory.

In retrospect I am less certain that my initial decision, mostly unexamined, was necessarily the appropriate one. Later when I decided to work on a totally unfamiliar issue, a school undergoing racial and ethnic transition, I discovered that creating a PBL project on this issue was exciting, informative, and much easier than I had anticipated. Moreover, the project consumed much less time than I had expected, closer to 120 than 160 hours. Whether my efficiency was due to my increased understanding of how to create a project, my strategy, or both, I will never know with certainty.

To develop a project on the issue of a school undergoing racial and ethnic transition, I first interviewed a number of principals and superintendents who had firsthand experience with this issue. Through these interviews, I hoped to obtain a sense of the problems that commonly arose during this transition. Once I had identified them, I proceeded to draft a case that embodied these problems. I then shared the draft with six experienced principals and asked them if the case seemed realistic. Their answer was a resounding "Yes."

Following my meeting with these principals, I then asked three members of the Stanford faculty (Kenji Hakuta, Amado Padilla, and John Baugh) to read the case and to suggest reading material that was relevant to the problems embedded in it. Much to my surprise, they identified a rich body of theory and research. I read this material plus other articles that knowledgeable practitioners (especially Kenneth Hill, superintendent of the Redwood City, California, School District) had found useful.

After perusing this set of materials, I chose references that would acquaint students with the theory and research in bilingual education, as well as school district policy and school programs that showed how theory and research had been translated into practice. The project, *In English, Please*, that emerged from these efforts appears in Appendix B.

Issue 2: What problems should be used, and how should they be presented?

Since there are an unlimited number of problems to choose from, on what basis might an instructor select from the vast array of problems? Although this question is a basic and important one, I have no definitive answer for it. When choosing focal problems for the problem-stimulated projects, I have juggled several concerns: a set of criteria that seemed appropriate for choosing such problems, the requirements of the state accrediting agency in California, and my own interests and self-perceived expertise.

The following criteria or guidelines may be used when selecting focal problems for problem-stimulated projects:

1. The problems should be representative of the kinds of problems students are likely to encounter in the roles and the contexts for which they are being prepared.

2. The problems should be suitable for integrating knowledge from a variety of disciplines (for example, law, social science, and education).

3. The problems should be ones that have high potential impact, that is, they affect large numbers of people for an extended period.

4. The problems should expose students to "discovered" and "presented" problems (Getzels 1970).

This last criterion seems especially critical and requires further amplification. The administrator who serves as the leader for tomorrow's schools must possess foresight and be able to anticipate the crucial problems that lie ahead, that is, be capable of discovering problems and solving them. There are at least three major types of discovered problems school leaders must be able to deal with:

- *the agenda for leadership* (sizing up a new situation, synthesizing the information that he or she has acquired, and using this information to create a pathway or vision for the future)

- *the improvement effort* (recognizing the opportunities that exist for attaining better results, developing a plan for capitalizing on these opportunities, and ensuring the successful implementation of these improvement efforts)

- *the future threat* (reading the current situation, foreseeing serious trouble that lies ahead, and instituting preventive actions to forestall the occurrence of the threat or instituting a contingency plan to minimize the negative consequences should the threat materialize)

Each of these three types of discovered problems is future-oriented and requires the administrator to be a proactive visionary rather than a fire fighter.

In order for administrators to be able to work on "discovered" problems, they must also be capable of dealing with "presented" problems. Otherwise, the administrators may become overwhelmed by the "presented" problems and, thereby, be robbed of the time and the energy to deal with the more creative side of leadership. Whereas the "discovered" problems emphasize problem-finding skills, the "presented" problems emphasize skills in problem-solving. The "presented" problems are in the here-and-now and require action because something is wrong and needs fixing.

"Presented" problems, like their "discovered" counterparts, come in several different forms, for example:

- *the swamp* (the generalized mess that is so complex that the administrator has real difficulty in getting a handle on what the problem is—sometimes referred to in terms like "the morale problem" or "the communications problem")

- *the dreaded problem* (the type of problem few administrators want to handle)

- *the routine, garden variety problem* (the type of problem an experienced administrator has encountered many times before and has developed an effective way of responding when it arises)

- *the dilemma* (the administrator knows what is wrong, and the problem is basically a choice among alternatives involving a sacrifice or tradeoff of important personal and/or organizational objectives)

- *the implementation problem* (the administrator is assigned a new policy or program to implement and must figure out how to ensure the successful implementation of this policy or program)

It should be noted that not all problems fit neatly into one of these categories; some problems may fit in none of these categories, while others may actually fall into two or more.

Once having chosen the problems to be included in a problem-stimulated project, the instructor must then decide how to present them. The focal problems can be presented as a written case, a live role play, an interactive computer simulation, an interactive video-disc presentation, or a taped episode.

Sole reliance on written cases or verbal vignettes, as Bransford and others (1989) have noted, may have dysfunctional consequences for the learner. For example, the medical student who is trained to make a diagnosis based on verbal vignettes may be at a loss when confronted with real patients. Since the verbal vignette itself is "the output of an expert's pattern recognition process" (Bransford and others 1989, p. 484), the student may not learn "to recognize symptoms like 'slightly defensive' and 'moderately depressed' on their own."

To become an expert, a great deal of perceptual learning must occur, and this cannot happen unless the student learns to recognize the salient visual, auditory, and nonverbal cues. When designing a PBL curriculum, program designers should strive for a variety of modalities in presenting problems to educational administrators. If students encounter only verbal descriptions of problems, they may be unprepared to deal with real problems.

Despite the soundness of Bransford's rationale and my efforts to follow it, I recognize that I have relied too heavily on one presentation mode. To be sure, problems are presented in a variety of modalities in the projects, but the dominant mode is the written case. In this regard, I have found it difficult, but not impossible, to follow Bransford's sensible advice. Perhaps others will be more successful than I have in acting on his admonition.

Issue 3: What kinds of products and product specifications should be included in a PBL project?

Products are indispensable features of a problem-based learning project for administrators. These products ensure that students will be forced to deal with a host of issues involved in getting results through others. Team products require students to reach group decisions, to confront varying views about what the problem is and how it should be handled, and to figure out how they should organize themselves to accomplish their product objective(s) within the time constraints. These products provide a focus for the team's efforts, an incentive for learning, and a means by which the leader and team members can judge the effectiveness of their efforts.

Some products by their very nature are individual, rather than group. Classroom observations and postobservation conferences are examples of such products; even these may be preceded by group discussion and planned with assistance from the team.

In creating products and drafting specifications for these products, instructors should strive to follow these guiding principles:

- Products should be representative of the kinds of products and performances inherent in the administrative role for which students are being prepared.

- Product specifications should encourage (or require) students to use the knowledge and skills they have learned in the current project or in previous projects.

- Product specifications should require students to take action and to grapple with issues of implementation.

- Product specifications should place students in situations where they experience the consequences of their own actions and the actions of other team members.

Constructing products and product specifications that meet these four guidelines poses a major challenge for the project designer. The fourth guideline, placing students in situations where they experience the consequences of their actions, is especially challenging. I have attempted to meet this guideline in a variety of ways, sometimes with only partial success.

For example, in the *Write Right!* project, I arrange for a superintendent to read the problem, to examine the memo that students prepare in response to the problem, and to provide them with his reactions to their memo. This arrangement provides students with some sense of the consequences of their actions. They learn what one superintendent's reactions are to their proposed plan; however, they have no sense of whether the plan will produce the desired outcomes if it is implemented.

In the *Present Your Case* project (see Appendix B), I arrange for three local school board members to read the focal problem and to role play the board of education in the case. These three members listen to the students' presentation, ask them questions about their proposed course of action, vote on whether to accept the students' recommendation, and provide them with immediate feedback about their performance. This particular arrangement affords students the opportunity to learn whether the board approves their recommendation; however, they have no way of knowing what problems they will encounter in implementing their recommendation if it receives board approval.

In some projects, I knowingly violate one or more of the guidelines, either to promote student learning or because I am unable to imagine how a guideline might be met. For example, in the *Meeting Management* project, I intentionally selected a product (and a focal problem as well) that was not representative of the products (or problems) confronted by administrators. During one of the field tests of this project, I discovered that more educationally relevant products (and problems) interfered with students achieving one of the major learning objectives, namely, learning how to use the interaction method to run meetings. When students were assigned a more relevant product (and problem), they became preoccupied with the content in the meeting and were less able to concentrate on the process. By creating a less relevant project (and problem), I was able to avoid this difficulty.

Even if one judges my guidelines to be sensible, applying them, as I have tried to show, is hardly straightforward. These guidelines point the way for choosing products and creating product specifications. Moreover, the product specifications for the projects included in this book illustrate how these guidelines may be met, wholly or in part. In the final analysis, however, designing a project that meets these guidelines depends in large measure on one's knowledge of practice, judgment, and imagination. Lacking one or more of these qualities, project designers may do as I have done. On several occasions, I have found it helpful to include practicing administrators in preparing the product specifications for a project. In retrospect, I wish that I had involved them in creating the specifications for all the projects.

Issue 4: What kinds of resources should be included in a problem-stimulated learning project?

Four major types of resources might be included in a problem-stimulated learning project: reading materials, consultants, videotapes, and audiotapes. Moreover, each of these types, like Baskin and Robbins ice cream, comes in different flavors; some of these flavors will become evident in the discussion that follows. Irrespective of type, *these resources, whenever possible, should expose students to relevant theory and research and provide examples of how this theory and research have been translated into school policy and practice.* Based on my experience with numerous problem-stimulated projects, adhering fully to this principle will be difficult because for many problems one or more of these ingredients (theory, research, and examples of school policy and practice) is usually missing.

When choosing reading materials, professors tend to rely on textbooks and journal articles. These materials can be supplemented with other types of publications, most notably materials produced by state departments of education, local school districts, and individual school sites. These publications are rich sources of school policies and practices that reflect practical wisdom or illustrate how theory and research have been or might be applied in the schools. Perhaps the single best example of how these types of publications have been used in the projects I have created is *In English, Please* (see Appendix B).

Consultants, generally professors and practitioners, may be incorporated into problem-stimulated projects in a variety of ways. Initially, I invited practitioners (personnel directors and principals) to consult with students while they worked on their projects. Consultants were prohibited from providing advice on how to handle a focal problem. Rather, they were encouraged to answer questions that students might raise in relation to the problem or to raise questions that might assist students in exploring aspects of the problem they might have overlooked.

Although students uniformly regarded the consultants as valuable resources, I saw several drawbacks. Since the program occurred in the summer, I often found it difficult to locate consultants who could be available when they were needed. Scheduling these consultants in advance also created other problems. Projects sometimes took more time than was allotted; changing the time schedule often cost us a consultant. In other instances, students found that they needed a consultant for a project at a time different from the scheduled one.

As a response to the scheduling problem, I experimented with a videotape format. We taped a panel of principals while they discussed how they would deal with a focal problem. I subsequently made this videotape available to students; they viewed it whenever they chose, either before or after deciding how they intended to resolve the problem. With this new format, I expected to achieve four objectives:

1. counteract the "one best decision" syndrome (practitioners rarely agreed on the solution)

2. foster the students' own self-confidence (they sometimes recognized facets of the problem overlooked by principals and glowed when their own solutions were mentioned by one or more of the principals)

3. increase students' sensitivities to issues that often come only through direct experience

4. expand their repertoire of possible solutions

Despite the poor sound quality of the earliest tapes, the four objectives were achieved. I later discovered an inexpensive Radio Shack microphone (Realistic, PZM, 33-1090-B) that produces superb sound quality.

Philip Hallinger has experimented with another format in a project called *Something Old, Something New, and the Principal's Blues.* He developed two videotapes that reflected perspectives from theory/research and practice. In one videotape he taped several authors of the reading materials included in the project (for example, Michael Fullan and Andrew Hargreaves) discussing their views about how the problematic situation should be approached. In the second videotape, two experienced principals (one male and one female) present contrasting views of how the principal should deal with the focal problem. These two tapes provide a rich set of supplementary resources for the project.

I also have produced several videotapes that demonstrate conferences with different types of "problem" teachers. During one of the supervision and evaluation projects, I role played a passive-aggressive teacher, a highly dependent teacher, and a teacher who fails to own his problem. Students in the practicum observed one of their colleagues conduct a conference with me as I role played one of these "problem" types. We videotaped these conferences so that other students could attempt to discern the pattern of behavior associated with each type, to examine how the "principal" was coping with the situation, to determine what happened when the principal behaved that way, and to explore other ways of coping with these types of "problem" teachers. (The students evidently found my role playing convincing because they presented me with an Oscar at the end of the summer.)

Besides these home-grown videotapes, I have also used some tapes that were produced commercially. Two tapes stand out as especially well done. One is *Setting the Tone*, a tape showing eight elementary and secondary teachers on the first day of school as they are setting the tone, discussing class rules, and explaining the consequences for breaking them. This tape warrants two thumbs up and is available from Agency for Instructional Technology (Box A, Bloomington, Indiana 47402). The second tape that I have found valuable is *Another Set of Eyes*. This tape demonstrates a number of classroom observation techniques described in Acheson and Gall (1987) and is available from the Association for Supervision and Curriculum and Development (125 North West Street, Alexandria, VA 22314-2798).

Issue 5: How important is it to field-test a problem-based learning project?

The answer to this question is unequivocal; it is absolutely essential to field-test a project. Despite my best efforts, I have never been able to create a flawless project. I have learned from every field-test and modified the project based on student feedback and my own perceptions of what went awry.

To solicit feedback from students, I have designed a "Talk Back" form. A copy of the original form appears in table 7.

For some projects, the student Talk Back sheets have been generally positive and suggested few, if any, changes. Even in those rare cases, I have observed ways in which the projects could be improved. Such was the case in the initial field-test of the project on meeting management. The student's comments reproduced in table 8 were representative of the feedback I received. These comments were generally supportive; criticisms tended to center on the usefulness of some of the readings.

Although the Talk Back from students suggested the need for few changes, I perceived two problems that might be alleviated by modifying the project. First, both groups stumbled, one substantially more than the other. I felt that this floundering was due in part to a lack of familiarity with problem-based learning. In response to this issue, I prepared an *Overview* that introduced stu-

---

TABLE 7

Talk Back Form to Solicit Student
Input About a Project

TALK BACK

We need your reactions to the learning project; these will play an important role in our decisions to modify, leave as is, or drop this project. Please let us have your candid reactions to what has occurred. We will take them seriously! Please write your comments on the back of this sheet if necessary.

1. How did you feel about the project when you first read about what it involved?

2. Now that you have completed the project, what are your feelings about it?

3. What did you learn from the project?

4. What effect, if any, is this project likely to have on your behavior in the future?

5. What recommendations would you make for improving this project? (If you feel that the project should be dropped, please indicate why you feel that way.)

---

dents to the practicum and the role PBL played in it. Second, one group performed much better than the other. Upon close inspection, I concluded that the performance differences were due to the exceptional skills of one of the group leaders. She conceptualized the exercise as a project from the outset and used a system of meeting management, the interaction method, to run the meetings.

These perceived differences between the functioning and the output of the two groups led me to institute several changes. I decided to refer to the PBL exercises as projects, to include readings on project management, and to replace some of the readings with a book on the interaction method. These changes led to improved performance by future groups in this project.

For other projects, the Talk Back from students has pointed to serious problems and has suggested ways in which the projects might be improved. By way of illustration, my first field-test of the project on time management, *It's About Time!*, almost flopped. The students made comments like the following:

TABLE 8

Student Talk Back from the Project
on Meeting Management

TALK BACK

We need your reactions to the learning project; these will play an important role in our decisions to modify, leave as is, or drop this project. Please let us have your candid reactions to what has occurred. We will take them seriously! Please write your comments on the back of this sheet if necessary.

1. How did you feel about the project when you first read about what it involved?

Answer: I looked forward to it.

2. Now that you have completed the project what are your feelings about it?

Answer: It was a satisfying learning experience and a great way to start in building a team out of our group. The level of success we experienced helped build trust and respect among group members. I thought it was a great beginning.

3. What did you learn from the project?

Answer: Some specific techniques and approaches for problem solving and meeting management.

4. What effect, if any, is this project likely to have on your behavior in the future?

Answer: I'll be aware of problem-solving techniques to use with groups where people don't know each other well or have a preexisting system for approaching challenges. Very good ways to build consent before moving into the heart of difficult or controversial issues/problems. It was very helpful to realize the advantage of the neutral facilitator and to contrast this with the disadvantage of being a facilitator-leader with a strong view. Difficult to achieve consensus after full participation if, as a leader, I think I know the "right" course and there is conflict in the group. I'll be aware of this in the future.

5. What recommendations would you make for improving this project? (If you feel that the project should be dropped, please indicate why you feel that way.)

Answer: The piece on groupwork seemed lightweight for a reader with more than a year of two of teaching experience. I think we all faced this issue long ago. "Social Distance" was self-evident to me. Grove's piece was interesting and held some new ideas. Ware's "How to Run a Meeting" was a helpful gathering of information about dealing with controversy.

"It was not very satisfying."

"It had more problems than the other ones. I had great frustrations."

"I thought we were part of a giant experiment—it seemed that everything that happened in the time this project was taking place was a deliberate test of our time management abilities! I definitely think it is an important topic to include, but circumstances conspired to make me feel the *need* for time management more than the *how* of it."

"It was a frustrating experience."

"The in-basket simulation was stressful."

Students also offered an extensive list of suggestions for improving the project. Several of the comments that led to changes in the project were as follows:

"Create a context for the simulation (that is, what would be our master plan, vision, values for a school we'd be principal of—how would this guide our decisions). Have the simulation for 1 and ¹/₂ hours instead of 3."

"An angry parent or upset teacher might add drama and reality to the situation."

"A shorter simulation (1 hour and a half?)."

"Allow at least one more meeting for this project. This will allow time for reading rather than skimming handouts for material which helps the product. Visits of experts don't need to be scheduled so tightly with the problem solving dimension of the project."

Comments like these enabled me to effect substantial improvements in the project and to make it one of the more interesting, satisfying projects for students.

Disseminating the Results

The final component of a possible strategy for overcoming the barriers that we identified earlier in this chapter involves dissemination. Most professors are judged in large part by their research and publications. Nontenured faculty are wont to refer to this expectation as "Publish or perish." As these same faculty age and acquire tenure, they come to realize that they will perish whether they publish or not. Despite this discomforting realization, many professors strive to publish until they perish or retire.

In the field of medical education, professors combine their interests in problem-based learning with their need to publish. The literature is filled with systematic empirical investigations that contrast the student outcomes associated with conventional and PBL instruction. Many of these studies appear in the Bibliography. The periodical literature also is filled with numerous accounts of how PBL has been incorporated into an entire curriculum or a particular course. Finally, medical educators have published workbooks (for example, R. Waterman and others, *Clinical Problem-Based Learning: A Workbook for Integrating Basic and Clinical Science*. Albuquerque: University of New Mexico Press, 1988) that become excellent resources for other universities. Clearly, there is ample evidence to suggest that it is feasible for professors of educational administration to wed their concern for teaching with their need to publish.

Summary

In this chapter I attempted to provide some insight into how PBL may be implemented in a higher education context. I identified some of the major barriers professors and departments are likely to encounter—the institutional reward system, the scarcity of resources (principally, time and money), and the attitudes and expertise of faculty.

As a way of overcoming these barriers, I suggested a four-stage strategy: (1) raising funds from external sources to initiate the program, (2) using materials developed elsewhere to assess student and faculty reactions to PBL, (3) developing PBL projects, and (4) disseminating the results to others. For each of the first three stages, I discussed what I had learned from my own attempts to create a PBL curriculum and cited numerous examples of these efforts. My intent in providing these examples was not to present them as models; rather, my purpose was much more modest—to provide the reader with a clearer picture of what was entailed in implementing a PBL curriculum.

To those readers who undertake the intellectual challenges inherent in moving from a traditional to a problem-based learning approach, I hope that you experience the same benefits that I and others have enjoyed—a renewed interest in teaching, an exciting opportunity to learn more about the problems of practice, and more positive feedback from students.

Based on our experience and informal discussions with other professors who are using PBL, I anticipate that professors will receive higher teaching evaluations from students in courses that employ problem-based learning. Some PBL users inform me that their student evaluations are higher than those professors who are teaching the same course using a traditional approach. Other users tell me that they received the highest student ratings in their career when they switched to PBL. Still others report more positive student ratings for their PBL-taught courses than their traditionally taught courses. If these experiences are replicated in other settings, students may one day point to departments of educational administration as exemplars of teaching and standard-bearers for quality instruction.

PBL: Future Challenges

For the past few years, I have devoted considerable time and effort to understanding how problem-based learning might be used in preparing administrators. To date, I have concentrated on explicating one version of PBL, problem-stimulated learning. As my attention turns to the future, I see four major challenges confronting those who are interested in exploring the role of PBL in teaching aspiring and experienced administrators. These challenges include: (1) explicating student-centered learning; (2) creating programs that prepare administrators to become independent, self-directed, lifelong learners; (3) conducting research on the effectiveness of PBL; and (4) exploring how PBL might be used in other contexts to educate administrators. My thoughts on these four challenges follow.

Student-Centered Learning

As I indicated in chapter 1, there are two major versions of problem-based learning: problem-stimulated and student-centered. These two versions differ primarily in terms of who selects the learning objectives and the learning resources. In problem-stimulated learning the instructor makes the choice, whereas in student-centered learning students decide. According to the proponents of

PBL, student-centered learning affords students a greater opportunity to develop some of the lifelong learning skills they will need after graduation, namely, skills in identifying their own learning needs and in locating resources that meet these needs.

Since student-centered learning promotes important learning objectives and has not been fully explicated as an instructional strategy, its utility in preparing administrators should be explored. Future explorations might take one of several forms. The first and simplest approach would involve transforming problem-stimulated projects into student-centered projects by omitting the learning objectives and the resources. Under this arrangement, students would read a project, decide on their learning objectives, and proceed to locate those resources most closely matching their self-defined learning needs. Projects that seem best suited for this transformation are ones with messy, ill-defined problems containing a variety of legal, economic, political, curricular, and organizational issues.

A second approach to student-centered learning might take the form of students working on current problems of practicing principals. Under this format, students meet with a school principal and a few members of her school staff. At this meeting the principal and her staff members provide background information about the school, its instructional program, their major goals for the coming year, and the challenges they face in trying to accomplish these goals.

Following this meeting with the principal and her staff, the students then decide on such matters as the following: the problem they will address, the learning issues that seem of greatest interest to them, and the product(s) they will complete in response to the problem. Once these decisions are made, students locate and examine the resources, share with one another what they have learned, and develop their product. When the product is completed, students again meet with the principal and her staff to discuss the product and to answer questions the product raises.

A third approach involves students in creating and field-testing a problem-stimulated learning project. This approach may be used in two different formats. A team of students can create a problem-stimulated project and implement it as a requirement for a course. Alternatively, students can work alone and use their projects to fulfill the dissertation requirement for the Ed.D. degree.

This second approach has been used at Vanderbilt University to complete the project *Something Old, Something New, and the Principal's Blues*.

Regardless of the approach used, project designers should anticipate that the learning objectives students select may not correspond to the ones mandated by state accrediting agencies. Medical educators who have designed student-centered learning modules with particular objectives in mind have discovered that there is some overlap between the instructor's and the students' objectives. The overlap, however, is far from perfect.

Lifelong Learning

One of the major goals of PBL is to promote skills in lifelong learning. Student-centered learning addresses this goal but in a limited fashion. There is more to lifelong learning than identifying one's learning needs and locating resources that match these needs. If administrators are to become independent, self-directed, lifelong learners, they will need a broader range of skills and knowledge than are typically emphasized in student-centered learning.

My own thinking on the issue of lifelong learning is in its formative stages and has been influenced by the work of Manning and DeBakey (1987). These two scholars have studied the continuing educational practices of physicians. Their work prompts questions like the following:

1. What are the obstacles to independent, self-directed learning by administrators?

2. How have and how might administrators overcome these obstacles?

3. What methods have administrators used or might they use in their quest to be lifelong learners?

4. What techniques and strategies have administrators used or might they use to maximize the benefits they receive from their self-study activities?

5. How have and how might administrators use the fruits of their self-study?

6. How do or might administrators model for others the importance of self-study?

7. How might administrators organize their own work in order to learn from experience and to plan their own program of continuing education?

This last question especially intrigues me. Manning and DeBakey (1987) found a number of physicians who studied their own professional practice and used the results to plan their own program of continuing self-development. Although I do not anticipate that there are many, if any, administrators who behave in this fashion, I am intrigued by the possibility and what might be learned from these pacesetters.

If such administrators do exist, it would be interesting to compare the practices of these administrators with the practices of the physicians studied by Manning and DeBakey (1987). Some of the physicians in their study logged the problems they encountered in their practice and designed a program of self-study to increase their understanding of their most commonly encountered problems. Other physicians recorded their mistakes in a "mistake book" as a means of learning from their errors and avoiding them in the future. Still other physicians systematically logged patient outcomes with a view toward understanding why some patients completely recovered and others did not. Each of these approaches has an analogue in administrative practice.

In meeting the challenges associated with designing a PBL curriculum to develop lifelong learning skills, designers might use a three-step strategy. First, they seek answers to the seven questions listed above. Second, they develop PBL projects that acquaint students with the range of practices and possibilities for independent, self-directed, lifelong learning. Finally, designers identify and develop the skills underlying the practices and the possibilities. If these challenges are met, the field of administration will move to the forefront of all professions in fostering independent, self-directed learning skills.

Research

Research is needed that probes the effectiveness of PBL in

preparing administrators. There are at least two distinct approaches that might be used in conducting this research. One follows the lead of medical educators and asks a variant of this basic question: *Do problem-based learning programs produce significantly better student outcomes than traditional programs?* The outcomes that might be studied include knowledge, administrative skills, problem-solving skills, lifelong learning skills, attitudes toward the instructional environment, approaches to studying, completion rates, perceived value of theory and research, and perceived relevance of the training.

The other approach asks a variant of the following question: *How effective are the various species of PBL in achieving the different goals of administrative preparation?* One might explore this question in several ways. By way of illustration, research might examine the differential effectiveness of problem-stimulated and student-centered learning in achieving the goals of the curriculum. Alternatively, research might focus on particular features of PBL. I have asserted that a product is an essential feature of a PBL project. It is indeed possible that a product is not as critical as I have presumed. Research could shed light on the validity of this presumption, as well as other presumptions (for example, the value of an integrative essay and the need for more than an overview of PBL to introduce students to this approach).

By following this second line of research, one would pit the different species of PBL against one another, rather than against traditional forms of preparation. When examining the effectiveness of these different species, the researcher would seek to discover which species were most effective in accomplishing certain types of goals. Some versions of PBL might be more effective in promoting administrative and problem-solving skills, while other versions might be more effective in promoting knowledge retention and use. Future research might investigate these possibilities.

Regardless of whether future research on PBL addresses a variant of the first or the second question, it seems important to avoid some of the problems inherent in the research conducted by medical educators. Research on the effectiveness of PBL in training physicians has followed the pattern observed in most program evaluations. Program evaluators have not tended to "describe fully, let alone measure, how the programs in 'experimental' and 'control' situations actually differ from one another—or even to certify that they do" (Charters and Jones 1975, p. 342). Researchers who examine the effectiveness of PBL in preparing administrators should define their programs with considerable precision and should certify that these programs actually operated as they were described.

When studying differences in medical knowledge, researchers generally measure the student's knowledge in cued contexts (that is, on examinations in which the student is provided with questions and alternative answers). Given the rationale for PBL, it seems far more reasonable to study whether *students spontaneously use the knowledge in noncued contexts* (Bransford and others 1989) *and whether they use the knowledge appropriately.*

Finally, medical researchers have shown little or no interest, thus far, in studying the effectiveness of PBL in promoting lifelong learning skills. The more emphasis that is placed on developing these skills in administrative preparation, the more important it is to study how PBL affects the inclinations of administrators to engage in lifelong, independent learning.

PBL in Other Contexts

At this point, I am tempted to claim that PBL can be used effectively in a variety of contexts. Since my experience with this instructional strategy is limited to a higher education context, I have chosen to forgo this claim. Instead, I think it is more reasonable to suggest several contexts in which PBL might be tried. If these field trials are actually conducted, they could yield valuable insights into the conditions under which PBL can be effectively used in achieving the goals of administrator education.

A number of medium- to large-size school districts operate their own inservice education programs for those teachers who aspire to be principals in the district. Given that the problems facing principals often vary across levels (elementary/middle/ high school) and settings (ethnic and social class), PBL seems ideally suited to acquaint prospective principals with the array of problems they may confront in their own districts. As the aspiring principals are exposed to these problems, they may further learn about the district-specific constraints and resources that are relevant to these problems. Additionally, the students may learn about the formal knowledge base that may be brought to bear on these problems.

If district officials wish to assess the administrative potential of each candidate, they can evaluate the performance of candidates in a variety of PBL project roles—team leader, facilitator, recorder, and member. I expect that school officials will be greatly surprised by what they learn about candidates as they enact these various project roles.

Virtually every district, irrespective of size, faces momentous issues and challenges that, if mishandled, may lead to serious, long-term, negative consequences. How should the district respond to a budget shortfall? How should a local school deal with a multilingual student population? How should the district handle school closure? How should the school respond to a state-mandated curriculum change? How should the district upgrade its instructional staff? When confronted with issues like these, a district may choose to frame them as learning opportunities as well as problems. By joining "here and now" problems with learning, district officials can design staff development programs that lead to more informed administrators and teachers. Equally important, these problem-based learning projects may also generate more effective responses to important, pressing district problems.

Many school districts release their administrators to participate in workshops and conferences that are conducted by other agencies. These settings provide another context in which PBL might be used. If workshops and conferences used a PBL approach, they would provide advance registrants with an overview of PBL and a copy of a problem-stimulated project, including the learning objectives and key reference materials. Once at the workshop or conference site, administrators would be assigned to project teams and be charged with the responsibility of creating a product to resolve the problem. One or two administrators who had experience in dealing with the focal problem would serve as resources to each project team. As resources, these "expert" administrators would not tell what they did to resolve the problem. Rather, they would raise questions that sensitize "novice" administrators to the issues that one is likely to be aware of only through firsthand experience.

The concluding session of each workshop or conference would provide participants with an opportunity to share their products with one another. Administrators crave opportunities to discuss common problems in nonthreatening settings, and this kind of format satisfies this craving and expands their practical and formal knowledge as well.

Summary

Four major challenges confront those who are interested in exploring the role of PBL in preparing administrators. First, although there are compelling reasons for using student-centered learning in administrator preparatory programs, this version of PBL remains unexplicated and untested. This chapter briefly describes three different ways in which this challenge might be confronted.

A second challenge centers on developing a curriculum that teaches administrators how to become independent, self-directed, lifelong learners. As a starting point for thinking about how this challenge might be met, I posed seven key questions. The answers to these questions might provide the basis for designing a curriculum that prepares administrators to be lifelong learners.

The effectiveness of PBL in preparing administrators remains unproven and unstudied. Research on this issue constitutes the third challenge. It may be approached by asking a variant of one or both of the following questions: Do problem-based learning programs produce significantly better student outcomes than traditional programs? How effective are the various species of PBL in achieving the different goals of administrator preparation?

The fourth and final challenge relates to how PBL may be used in contexts other than higher education to prepare administrators. Three possibilities were suggested: district-sponsored training programs for administrative aspirants, district-sponsored staff development programs built around major problems facing the district, and workshops and conferences sponsored by external agencies.

The Prospective Principals' Program at Stanford

In designing the Prospective Principals' Program at Stanford University, we confronted the following major issues:

1. What should be the program goals?
2. What should be the curricular content of the program?
3. How should the program be staffed?
4. How should problem-based learning be incorporated into the program?
5. How should the program be structured?
6. How should students be recruited and selected?
7. How should the program be evaluated?

The discussion that follows describes how we initially resolved these important design questions and what we learned that prompted us to institute changes in our original design.

Program Goals

At the outset of our deliberations, we set ourselves a challenging intellectual task. We deemed it important to establish one major goal that would enable us to make subsequent decisions about what the content of the program should be and how the program should be staffed. After agonizing several months about the nature of this goal, we settled on the following: to prepare principals who can lead people and can manage ideas (most notably, teaching, learning, subject matter, and the social context of schooling), things, and self in order to achieve results for a diverse student population. During the early stages of the planning process, we relied heavily on this stated goal as we fleshed out the details of the program.

Although this goal statement proved useful in making staffing and curriculum decisions, we later learned that it did not fully reflect the realities of what was actually occurring in the program. Through external evaluations of the program conducted by the Center for Teaching and Learning at Stanford University, we learned that the *operational goal* of the program was more like the following:

> to prepare principals to use a collaborative approach with parents, students, and faculty in solving problems, in establishing a high quality educational program for a diverse student population, and in creating a humane environment.

Moreover, through the evaluations we came to appreciate the need to model these same qualities in the staff's own behavior—acting collaboratively in identifying and solving problems within the program, offering an educational program of high quality, and creating a humane environment. We have subsequently revised the goal statement to reflect the operational goal and publicly declared the importance of modeling these goals in our own behavior.

Program Staffing and Content

Although the staffing and content of the program are analytically distinct, in actuality they are mutually interdependent. Faculty members possess expertise and interests that shape the content of the courses they are willing and able to teach. Therefore, choices about professors and course content are intertwined. Accordingly, we discuss these two issues together.

The curriculum that resulted from juggling faculty passions and expertise, state credentialing requirements, client preferences, personal convictions, and program goals reflects the contributions of a strong and diverse faculty. Both the faculty and the coursework (see the sidebar on pages 119-20) are representative of the various social science and education disciplines within the School of Education.

In addition to the coursework, students also are required to take a practicum and an internship. Each internship is individually tailored to reflect the student's background and career interests. Ordinarily, students have field experiences at two levels (elementary, middle, and high school). One of the assignments must be at a school with an

Courses, Faculty, and Disciplines Represented in the Prospective Principals' Program

Instruction of Socially Heterogeneous Populations (Elizabeth Cohen; Sociology). This course examines the challenges facing schools having multilingual, multiracial, and multicultural populations, with emphasis on critical evaluation of problem statements and proposed solutions. The role of the principal in promoting innovations designed to address these challenges is emphasized. Issues related to leadership for staff support and training as well as program coordination are discussed.

Understanding Cultural Differences (George and Louise Spindler; Anthropology). This course presents the principles and procedures of ethnography, with particular attention to its suitability as a method for the study of schools. Participants gain understanding of their personal cultural knowledge and its influence on perception and interpretation of ethnographic results.

The Role of Personality and Emotions in Organizations (Carl Thoresen; Psychology). This course presents theories of personality development and the nature of emotions, with particular emphasis on leadership skills relevant to maintaining productive interpersonal relationships in schools. Strategies for managing problems such as personality disorders and Type A behavior are discussed.

The Analysis of Teaching (Eliott Eisner; Art and Curriculum). This course presents various frames for the analysis of teaching, with emphasis on the implications for the principal's role as supervisor of instruction. Participants analyze how teaching is shaped by the structure of the school, cultural expectations, and curriculum.

The Role of Knowledge and Learning in Teaching (Lee Shulman, Psychology; Denis Phillips, Philosophy). This course examines the teaching process through a review of the concepts of the structure of knowledge in the disciplines and the insights of cognitive psychology. Participants apply these principles to the analysis of case studies of classroom teaching, to relevant issues in curriculum reform (higher order skills, depth vs. breadth of coverage), and to the construction of a plan for instructional improvement in a school.

Effective Schools: Research, Policy, and Practice (Larry Cuban; History and Administration). This course critically examines the research on effective schools since 1965, including discussion of the influence of teachers, principals, district superintendents, school boards, parents, and state and national policy-makers. Research methodologies, results of studies, and efforts to implement results are studied and critiqued. Participants develop their own definition of effectiveness and analyze the performance of a school or classroom based on their criteria.

School-Based Decision Making (Henry Levin; Economics). This course presents critical issues in developing a school-based decision-making model, with special emphasis on improving education for at-risk children. Participants use the Accelerated Schools Model to simulate the process of school improvement planning and to explore the impact of decentralized decision-making on the roles of the school board, administration, principal, staff, and parents. Research on the effectiveness of school-based decision-making models is presented.

Politics of Education (Michael Kirst; Political Science). This course explores the political process as it is carried out in school systems and in state and national education policy debates. The nature of interest groups, political strategies, community power, the external environment of organizations, and implementation of policy are discussed. Participants use various models of policy formulation to analyze educational reforms at the local, state, and national levels.

Curriculum: A Policy Focus (Decker Walker; Curriculum). Participants study issues related to curriculum development, implementation, and evaluation, and apply these principles in discussion of current curricular innovations. Problems addressed focus on the school principal's role in curricular decisions, including: assessment of the curriculum as presented in a classroom, evaluation of proposed curricular innovations, and planning for implementation of curricular change.

Note: All courses are taken for three units (quarter).

ethnically and socially diverse student body. A professor (a former superintendent of a district with an ethnically and socially diverse student population) and a building principal jointly supervise the intern. During the internship, each student constructs a portfolio that documents his or her experiences and accomplishments in the field.

Problem-Based Learning in the Principals' Program

There are at least four ways in which PBL can be incorporated into a curriculum for preparing educational administrators: (1) PBL can be used as the main instructional approach for the entire curriculum; (2)

the curriculum can consist of two tracks with one of these tracks using PBL as the main approach; (3) one or more courses in the curriculum can be organized around problem-based learning; and (4) a portion of one or more courses can use PBL. We chose the third option, organizing one or more courses around problem-based learning.

We elected this option for several reasons. First, using problem-based learning as the main instructional approach for the entire curriculum seemed foolhardy. PBL is untested and unproven in preparing educational administrators. Moreover, few of our current faculty are familiar with the basic tenets and practices of this approach. Second, offering a dual track with one track using PBL as the main approach seemed infeasible even if faculty were familiar with this instructional strategy and were willing to try it. Given our high tuition and admission standards, we believed that there would be too few students to fill two tracks. Third, we already had experimented with problem-based learning in a course; based on this experience, we seemed ready to organize the equivalent of one or more courses around the concept.

Having chosen this option, we further decided to use PBL as the major instructional strategy for 40 percent of the total curriculum. This decision led to a herculean undertaking; it meant designing the equivalent of six three-unit courses under the umbrella of a practicum. With a grant from the Walter S. Johnson Foundation, we were able to devote nearly one year to designing the practicum and the problem-based learning projects that formed its core. The fruits of our labor and what we have learned about PBL in preparing administrators are described in this book.

Program Structure

Whereas most students in educational administration work full-time and pursue their degrees in the evening on "tired time," students in the Stanford program study full-time for three consecutive summers. Courses are repeated every third year, which means that students, regardless of whether they are in the first, second, or third year of the program, generally take the same set of courses each summer. In addition, students participate in a field experience during the regular academic year.

We chose this pattern of study as a solution to four problems. First, faculty at Stanford hesitate to offer service courses on a regular basis. Few, if any, faculty members would choose to commit themselves to a program that involves teaching the same course every summer. Second, Stanford is a private university with extremely high tuition and admission standards. Under these circumstances, we anticipated that only a small number of students would be admitted each year. For the program to be cost-effective, we needed to create a structure that would produce course enrollments of fifteen to twenty students.

Third, we were interested in attracting students who were talented and dedicated teachers. During the program design phase we interviewed mentor teachers. We were somewhat surprised to discover that many of them had an interest in administration but were not pursuing certification because the evening courses interfered with their teaching commitments.

Finally, Stanford conceives of itself as an international university and desires to prepare individuals from all parts of the world, not just the Bay Area of California. By offering most of the training in the summer, we have a greater potential to serve a substantially larger geographical area. Full-time study in the summer with courses being repeated every third year solved all four of these problems.

During each of the first two summers, students took three courses and a practicum concurrently. This arrangement created a serious problem for students. Despite our belated efforts to coordinate the reading and writing assignments, students sometimes experienced overloading. When the loads became excessive, students understandably cut corners; as a result, their learning and understanding of the material suffered.

As a response to this problem, we decided on a trial basis to teach the three courses consecutively, rather than concurrently. This decision meant that at any given point during the summer quarter students would be taking only one course plus the practicum. After trying this arrangement for one quarter, we found that it solved the overload problem. Moreover, students and faculty alike preferred the new pattern by a wide margin. Typical summer and weekly schedules for students in the Prospective Principals Program appear in figures A1 and A2.

Recruitment and Selection

Historically, most programs in educational administration have not aggressively recruited students, nor have these programs been selective in whom they have admitted. Nearly 90 percent of the students, largely self-selected, are admitted (Alkire 1978); the vast majority of those who enroll eventually graduate.

FIGURE A1

Typical Eight-Week Schedule for Students in the Prospective Principals Program

Eight weeks

6/25-7/1	7/15-7/30	7/31-8/15
Course 1	Course 2	Course 3

←——————————— Practicum ———————————→

FIGURE A2

Typical Weekly Schedule for Students in the Prospective Principals Program

	Monday	Tuesday	Wednesday	Thursday
9:00-11:30	←——————————— Course 1 ———————————→			
1:15-4:05	1st yr practicum	2nd/3rd yr practicum	1st yr practicum	2nd/3rd yr practicum

Recruitment

In designing the Prospective Principals' Program, we chose to mount a comprehensive recruitment effort. To identify candidates for the first cohort, we wrote letters to the principals and superintendents of all school districts in the Bay Area. This letter announced the program and invited nominations of promising candidates.

In the second year, we tried a different approach. We met individually with the superintendents of six local school districts with a large population of students from socially and economically disadvantaged backgrounds. During this meeting, we explained the program and solicited nominees.

Our third effort involved visitations to six more school districts, written letters to a handful of superintendents with close ties to the School of Education, and letters to all individuals who had graduated from the Stanford Teacher Education Program during the past fifteen years. We also enlisted the efforts of current students in the program.

Through these efforts we have learned a great deal about recruitment. Although we reached and exceeded our enrollment targets each year, we discovered that our initial efforts to recruit minorities failed. On the assumption that the tuition posed special problems for this group (namely, they were more likely to be in debt for their undergraduate education and they were less likely to receive financial assistance from their families), we instituted a scholarship program during the second year. Most of the students who qualified for this financial assistance were targeted minorities (African-Americans and Hispanics). In the two years that this assistance program has been in effect, minority admissions have risen from zero to 33 percent.

We also have a better sense of what recruitment strategy produces the greatest payoff. Students in the program appear to be the most dependable and best sources of promising candidates. As we expand the number of school districts with students in our program, we anticipate that our current and former students will eventually become our major recruiters in the Bay Area.

In the near future we intend to mount a national recruitment program. Since we already have attracted students from Los Angeles, New Hampshire, and Nevada, we are optimistic that our national recruitment efforts will be successful.

Selection

Students who are admitted into the Prospective Principals' Program survive a four-stage process. In stage 1, an Admissions Committee consisting of three to four faculty members reviews each application with one overriding question in mind: Is this applicant capable of satisfactorily completing his or her graduate work at Stanford? Faculty members base their judgment on several sources of information: transcripts of previous college work, performance on the Graduate Record Examination, recommendations, and the candidate's own statement of purpose.

If the Admissions Committee decides that the candidate is capable of completing graduate work at Stanford, the applicant moves to stage 2, the interview. Two faculty members interview each applicant separately for approximately one hour; the interviews are structured with two major objectives in mind. One is to assess the candidates' motivation, sociability, and ability to express themselves. (See the sidebar on page 126 for a sample interview protocol.) The other objective is to stimulate in the candidate a strong desire to enter the program if he or she is admitted.

Following the interviews, successful applicants are, wherever possible, observed teaching a lesson. In some cases, the applicant submits a videotape of a lesson; in other instances, we view the applicant teaching in his or her own classroom. Each applicant also submits a written critique of the lesson. This critique generally contains the following features: a statement of the objective(s) for the lesson, a description of how the lesson fits into the curriculum, a description of the instructional strategy being used, an analysis of the strengths and weaknesses of the lesson, and a discussion of how and why the person might teach the lesson differently in the future. We attempt to judge the adequacy of the teacher's performance in relation to the stated objectives of the lesson, the teacher's skill in using the instructional strategy, and the teacher's own insight into the quality of his or her own teaching performance.

Applicants who reach the fourth and final stages of the selection process undergo a reference check. This stage serves two purposes. First, it enables us to assess how effectively the candidate works with adults and to determine if he or she has any glaring weaknesses. Second, this reference check is an occasion for us to obtain a commitment from the district to arrange a meaningful field experience for the applicant if he or she is admitted to the program.

During the three years this selection process has been followed, the percentage of successful applicants has ranged from 40 to 85 percent. All of the admittees have subsequently enrolled in the program.

Program Evaluation

Since the inception of the Prospective Principals' Program in 1989, we have conducted four evaluations of the program with two major objectives in mind: (1) to identify how the program might be improved and (2) to determine how satisfied students were with the program. Two of these evaluations were conducted in the fall following each of the first two summers of the program. The Stanford University Center for Teaching and Learning conducted both of these evaluations.

Two other evaluations were completed in the middle of the second and third summers. In one instance, the Center for Teaching and Learning conducted the evaluation and shared the results with the

Sample Interview Protocol

PART I

1. Why at this point in your career did you decide to enter a program to prepare yourself to become a principal? (Why do you want to be a principal?)

2. Why did you choose Stanford? (Are you intending to apply anywhere else? What do you hope to get out of program—personally? professionally?)

3. The program is quite demanding. You can expect to spend 15 hours per week in class and up to 30-35 outside. Are you prepared to spend that kind of time for 8 weeks for each of the next 3 summers?

4. Participation in the program also entails meeting once a month in the evening with other participants during the regular school year and time to work on projects related to your training during the regular year (might average 4-5 hours per week). Does this pose any problems for you?

5. The job of a principal demands long hours; are you sure that you are ready to spend that kind of time to get the job done?

PART II

1. People come in lots of different flavors. What types of people do you find it easiest to work with? What types of people do you find it difficult to work with or accept?

2. What kinds of colleagues don't you like? What about them don't you like? How do you relate to them?

3. Think of a time when you found yourself in conflict with someone else. What was the nature of the conflict? How did you deal with it? What was the outcome?

4. Most people have some weaknesses or shortcomings. What types of failings are easiest for you to accept? What types of failings do you find it nearly impossible to accept no matter how hard you try?

5. Do you have any bedrock values that you are unwilling to compromise under any conditions? What are they?

program director. He, in turn, met individually with each faculty member to discuss what the center had learned about the professor's course. In the other instance, the faculty assumed responsibility for conducting the midcourse evaluations. Besides these four program evaluations, we evaluated each unit in the practicum all three summers.

To provide the reader with a sense of how these evaluations were conducted, what we learned from them, and how we changed the program in light of these assessments, let us consider the first program evaluation in detail. Excerpts from this evaluation appear in the sidebar on pages 128-31; the report describes how the evaluation proceeded and what was learned.

After receiving this evaluation, the director gathered additional data to understand why students experienced such a high level of intensity and stress in the program and discussed these matters with the faculty who would be teaching in the program the following summer. Prior to meeting with each faculty member, the director asked faculty to read the memo in the sidebar on pages 132-33:

As a result of the meetings between faculty and the director regarding the issues raised in the program evaluation, several changes were instituted. The faculty met and jointly developed a program schedule listing the due dates for all written assignments in the courses and the practicum. Students received this schedule during the orientation held the day before classes began. Faculty also decided to create a set of course demands that were more reasonable in light of the total load being carried by students.

In an effort to obtain a more diverse student body, we established a partial-tuition scholarship program and changed our recruitment strategy. The recruitment plan used in the second year is described above under Recruitment.

These changes, along with the ones made to improve the practicum, evidently were successful. The program evaluation conducted after the second year produced the following comments by the evaluator:

Participants currently seem very happy with the program; there does not seem to be as much need this time around to express concerns. Instead, there is a high level of satisfaction, especially since the second year group felt needed improvements had already been made.

Summary

In this Appendix I have described how we resolved seven major

Evaluation of the Program for
Prospective Principals, Fall 1989

BACKGROUND

At Professor Ed Bridges' request, on October 16, 1989 [the day before the 7.1 Loma Prieta earthquake], I met with five of the first six participants in the Stanford School of Education Program for Prospective Principals (PPP). My purpose was to interview the five as a group regarding their evaluation of the program thus far. Although the setting and tone were deliberately informal, the interview was structured along the lines of a teaching evaluation technique called Student Small Group Evaluation. Whereas our purpose in teaching situations is to determine what students like about a class, what they think needs improvement, and how they would implement the improvements, here my purpose was to determine the group's major satisfactions with the program thus far, their major disappointments, and the surprises, positive and negative. I also indicated to the group that I wanted them to feel as if they too would benefit from this evaluation and that they should therefore tell me what they hoped to get from it.

I then divided the five participants into two groups and gave each group approximately ten minutes to discuss among themselves the areas outlined above. Only after each group had had some time to talk amongst themselves did I bring us all together and go systematically through the major headings outlined below. My task at that point was to pose the questions, keep discussion on track, listen for implicit as well as explicit themes in the responses, and *guarantee the anonymity of individual replies* [emphasis added]. The group showed itself to be overwhelmingly eager and willing not only to discuss their reactions but to be frank about them. We talked spiritedly for over ninety minutes and called a halt then only because of another commitment of the group members.

MAJOR SATISFACTIONS

After I had brought the two groups back together, we began by going over what each group had decided were the major areas of their satisfaction. Points are listed in the order in which the groups originally presented them. As it turned out, the two groups were unanimous in their responses with the one exception noted below.

As much as possible, I have also used the participants' own language and terms in stating the points.

- *The group itself.* (They hadn't expected to get so much from each other.)
- *That the faculty who taught them were aware of their participation in the PPP.* They liked the fact that faculty took note of and appreciated the practical experience of the PPP participants.
- *That most of the work was collaborative* (again a big and pleasant surprise).
- *That what they learned was relevant, interesting, and stimulating.*
- *The practicum.* This was the only point on which group members significantly disagreed. One loved the practicum, two were very enthusiastic about it, although they felt there were some problems, especially in the last one. Two thought it was essential and valuable but still had a lot of reservations. The practicum was discussed further under the next category.
- *That the faculty teaching them were of extremely high caliber*, the "cream of the crop."

MAJOR DISAPPOINTMENTS

Again, these are presented in the order in which the participants raised them and again there was great unanimity, except as noted. At my request, group members also discussed how they thought the disappointments might be addressed.

[Most centered on the practicum; these are reproduced below.]

- *Not enough time with Ed,* especially not enough time with him debriefing the practicum. The members of both groups agreed that this problem arose not because Ed was inaccessible—in fact, all agreed he was very generously accessible—but that students didn't have enough time to take advantage of his availability.

Possible solutions: have one less private session with Ed and involve him more in the practicum; have fewer projects, leaving more unstructured time to spend on each project and thus with the whole group and Ed; delay the last project to the second year and/or modify the first project to be a presentation rather than a project.

- *Mixed messages from Ed* about each of the groups working on a project, creating a sense of competition. Participants somehow felt that the other group was always doing better than their own; they were always "waiting for the other shoe to drop."

Possible solutions: Meeting as one group at the end of every project; realizing that some things Ed said to relieve performance anxiety may have actually contributed to it.

MAJOR SURPRISES

Pleasant ones:

- *Stanford's atmosphere:* personal, helpful, and professional; more heterogeneous than people had imagined it would be; a good place to learn; a friendly support staff.
- *Being allowed to collaborate.*

Not-so-pleasant ones:

- *The intensity of the program.* Most participants reported working at least eighty hours a week; one reckoned it at ninety. Three participants said that the intensity had made them think a lot about whether they wanted to continue with PPP and, indeed, whether they wanted to go in a career direction that also promises this level of intensity. As of the October 16th meeting, however, all participants said that they *would* be staying in the program.

WHAT PARTICIPANTS WOULD LIKE TO GET OUT OF THE EVALUATION:

- *That next summer is more manageable* in terms of the time demands.
- *That this year's group get to meet and talk early on* (as early on as possible) *to next year's entering class.*
- *That next year's group be more diverse.* Participants suggested that to achieve diversity they be invited to recruit for the program and that publicity should go directly to teachers (the participants could assist in targeting people).

EVALUATOR'S OBSERVATIONS

Although this group was able to identify some disappointments and unpleasant surprises in the PPP, their overall reaction is beyond doubt a very positive one. They were eager to talk, very quick to identify major areas of satisfaction, and full of appreciation for much of what they had experienced. They spoke especially warmly about the faculty who have taught them, the non-PPP students in the classes, Stanford as an institution, and each other. They also feel that the program is challenging and enriching them in significant ways.

Clearly, this is a successful program thus far. Two areas seem worthy of additional attention, however.

The first is the palpably high intensity of the program. All participants, with one possible exception, feel it in a very stressful way....

Closely allied to this concern is the obvious preoccupation among members of the group with their success as students. Although they are all established professionals already, it is clear that they are suffering great performance anxiety about the program....

If these two areas can be addressed, then not only would participant satisfaction levels rise and stress levels decline, but participants may also learn more of the behaviors that are necessary to successful principals.

Evaluator: Dr. Michele Marincovich, Assistant Dean of Undergraduate Studies and Director, Center for Teaching and Learning

issues in designing the Prospective Principals' Program. The program design that emerged differs substantially from modal practices in the field of educational administration. Underlying the program is one major goal: to prepare future principals to use a collaborative approach with parents, students, and faculty in solving problems, in establishing a high quality educational program for a diverse student population, and in creating a humane environment. Faculty and staff strive to model these same qualities in their own behavior.

The staff actively recruit students and use a rigorous four-stage process to evaluate applicants. Faculty members come from a broad range of social science and education disciplines within the School of Education. Course content emphasizes leadership, self-management, and the commonplaces of education (teaching, learning, curriculum, and social context).

Problem-based learning is used as the chief instructional strategy in 40 percent of the program. Students attend full-time, not part-time, for three consecutive summers.

During the first three years of its operation, the program has been extensively evaluated with two major objectives in mind: (1) to determine the students' level of satisfaction with the program and (2) to identify areas of the program needing improvement. These evaluations have led to several major changes in the program and in the problem-based learning component of the program.

Memo to Faculty re: Program Evaluation

To: (Name of faculty member)

From: Ed Bridges

I would like to talk with you about your summer course for the prospective principals' program. Please phone me after you read what follows as there is a serious problem that we must address as we plan our courses. This problem is how to create a manageable workload for the students in the program.

BACKGROUND

The day before the earthquake the Center for Teaching and Learning conducted a program evaluation with students at my suggestion. Results follow:

What they liked best about the program

- The fact that faculty took note of, appreciated, and valued the practical experience of PPP participants
- What they learned was relevant, interesting, and stimulating
- The faculty was of extremely high caliber
- Most of the work was collaborative

What they found to be unpleasant

- Intensity of the program; spent 80-90 hours most weeks on the program; made them think a lot about whether to continue in PPP
- Suffered great performance anxiety

What they want to get from the program evaluation

- A more manageable workload
- A more diverse group of students (namely, minorities)

CENTRAL ISSUE: A more manageable set of time demands with the workload they will be carrying during the eight-week period (three three-hour courses plus a six-hour practicum).

To obtain a clearer understanding of this issue, I personally interviewed several students, talked with the three professors who taught in the program last summer, and reviewed the syllabi and requirements for each course. There is no doubt in my mind that the students were overloaded. The following factors seemed to have contributed to this overload:

1. In some courses the due dates for the written assignments were not made clear until the last minute (this uncertainty made it difficult, if not impossible, for students to do sensible planning).

2. In some instances major written assignments were due at the same time in two or more of the courses.

3. In some courses there was little, if any, connection or overlap between the readings and the outside written projects/assignments, adding to the workload.

4. In one course the reading was in the students' words "intemperate."

What might be done to produce a more manageable workload

(that is, closer to sixty hours per week, fifteen hours in class plus three hours work outside class for each hour in class)?

1. Professors let students know at the beginning of the quarter what the major writing projects/assignments are for the quarter and either (a) specify the due dates or (b) allow the students to decide for themselves when they will submit the written projects/assignments.

If professors decide to specify the due dates, I should be provided with the due dates and look across the courses to see if the major writing assignments are piling up on certain dates. If so, we will need to consider how to address the problem.

2. Professors distinguish between required and optional readings and limit the required readings in each course to roughly nine hours per week—less if the major writing assignments are not tightly linked to the required readings.

3. Professors limit the group activities which require students to meet outside the regularly scheduled class hours.

4. Professors provide reading lists in March so that students can begin their reading before the summer (suggestion from students).

5. Other possibilities (your suggestions)?

[**NOTE:** It is important to bear in mind that students want and expect to be challenged; the problem is an overwhelming workload. We need to realize that they are taking five courses in eight weeks rather than the two or three courses in ten weeks taken by most of our doctoral students. Last year's group was a pleasure to work with—eager, bright, conscientious, and lively. I am optimistic that you will find your experiences similarly rewarding.]

SECONDARY ISSUE: Performance anxiety

Possible course of action: In each course we seek to provide students with some idea of how they are doing by the second or third week of the quarter. Other???

I look forward to meeting with you and getting your views on the issues raised by the program evaluation.

Examples of Problem-Stimulated Learning Projects for a PBL Curriculum

PRESENT YOUR CASE

Introduction

Contemporary research on the structure and workings of the brain—on attention span, the limits of memory, stages of mental development, and the way we use language—is providing new approaches to planning and delivering successful presentations. To reach and move an audience, an effective speaker must develop rapport, engage and tap the resources of the audience members, and create experiences that will motivate and support learning.

According to those who think about thinking, learning is more than the simple acquisition of facts. It is that elusive *change of mind* which results in new attitudes and behavior. Whether presentation content deals with information transfer, training, entertainment, or persuasion, this change of mind is the goal....

A state-of-the-art presentation is the product of a person who knows where and how to lead an audience; one who can recognize landmarks, shortcuts, and unexpected delight along the road; and one who knows when the group has reached its destination.... Excellent presenters interact with the highest potential of each person in the group. The skills that make this possible go beyond the category of technique. As they become second nature, these skills influence [the] ability to communicate effectively in all settings.

(From S. Berry & R. Garmston, "Become a State-of-the-Art Presenter," *Training and Development Journal*, January, 1987.)

This project was developed by the Center for the Advanced Study of Educational Leadership, Peabody College, Nashville, Tennessee 37203.

Work activity studies of the school principal consistently find a heavy reliance on the verbal medium; simply put, principals talk a lot. The ability to communicate effectively is an essential skill for every principal. Although principals engage in one-on-one communication throughout the day, they must frequently make presentations to groups. These presentations span a range of formats and audiences. They include a status report to the board of education, an informational presentation to the Parent-Teachers Organization, an entertaining speech at a retirement dinner or an awards assembly, a persuasive address to the superintendent's cabinet, or an instructional demonstration at a staff meeting or staff development session.

The audience, the goal of the presentation, and the nature of the content influence the speaker's approach and delivery. An astute presenter once observed that there are three keys to a successful presentation: **audience, audience, audience**. The presenter must remain mindful of the needs, predispositions, and resources of the audience at all times in order to maintain rapport. *Speaking to the converted* represents a very different set of tasks, in preparation and delivery, from *entering a pool of sharks*. Successful presenters maintain contact with their audience through a variety of verbal and nonverbal cues, as well as through the messages communicated by the structure of the presentation.

The **goal of the presentation** also shapes the manner in which information is presented. This project differentiates between two types of presentations: informational and persuasive. **Informational presentations** seek to communicate information in the absence of a stated point of view. Informational presentations are often (poorly) made at staff meetings. Informational presentations seem straightforward; it is this characteristic that often leads presenters to be lax in their preparation. Informational presentations should be approached with the mindset of effective teaching and learning. As you shall see, even informational presentations can become powder kegs when the nature of the content is highly charged.

The goal of **persuasive presentations** is to influence the audience to accept or adopt a particular point of view. Researchers have found that presenters who engage the audience in a series of specific steps in the presentation and discussion of ideas are more successful at persuading the audience to accept their point of view. Again, this becomes more difficult when the audience represents a variety of perspectives.

Finally, the **nature of the content** being delivered in the presentation must be considered, particularly in relation to the audience. Is the audience likely to be receptive, skeptical, disinterested, angry? How will their attitude be influenced by the content of the presentation? Long faculty meetings dominated by the principal's one-way delivery of information sap the energy of staff and lead them to apathy and disengagement. Effective speakers capitalize on the motivation and energy of the audience and shape the delivery of content in order to engage members of the audience to meet the presenter's goals.

Of course, speaking before an emotionally charged or skeptical audience about a controversial subject makes even the most seasoned speaker anxious. While no amount of instruction will alleviate this anxiety, you can learn skills that will make you a more effective public speaker. This learning project has as its primary objective the introduction and application of several presentation styles. Secondary objectives are to understand factors that influence curriculum selection decisions and to appreciate some of the issues concerning a highly controversial topic facing schools today—AIDS education.

Learning Objectives

1. Compare and contrast selected presentation styles and evaluate which situations are appropriate for each style.
2. Develop and deliver two individual presentations using one or more of the three presentation styles.
3. Perform an audience analysis.
4. Critique, in a positive and supportive manner, the video presentations of other group members.
5. Describe the process of curriculum selection and identify the rationale for selecting a particular curriculum.
6. Analyze the latest research on AIDS education.

Guiding Questions

1. How does the controversial nature of a presentation affect the preparation and delivery of a presentation?
2. What constitutes a good (and bad) presentation?
3. What circumstances contribute to an effective presentation?
4. What impact does a potential audience have on the organization and nature of a presentation?
5. What skills, knowledge, and attitudes must a presenter have in order to be effective in the delivery of a controversial presentation?
6. What kinds of issues influence the choice of a curriculum?
7. What impact do personal values of constituent groups have on curricular selection?

8. What effect do the personal values of the instructor have on his or her ability to teach controversial subjects?

The Problem

Cleburne is a rural community of about 15,000 people. Its economy has been chiefly dependent on agriculture and publishing. The primary crop is tobacco. The publishing industry is dominated by an evangelical denomination that has a wide following in the Southeast. The quaint downtown area boasts a lovely square and Confederate Monument, fifteen churches, a library, and an assortment of shops. These shops include a hardware store, a drugstore with lunch counter, a grocery store, a Five and Dime, and a once magnificent Art Deco movie house. Surrounding the central part of Cleburne are many lovely old houses, some dating back to before the Civil War. In fact, until recently, the atmosphere and pace around Cleburne had changed little since just after what some town folks term "The War of Northern Aggression."

Over the past seven years several factors brought an influx of new families to Cleburne. To accommodate the new arrivals, Cleburne has experienced a building boom. These new families have come in part to escape the pressures of city life, preferring to commute into, rather than live in, the nearest city, which is twenty miles to the west. An influx of new residents have come to help staff a facility built by a foreign corporation that manufactures silicon wafers used in telecommunications equipment.

The town of Cleburne has not completely adjusted to the rapid changes brought by so many newcomers to the area. These outsiders have brought new ideas and ways of doing things. The conflict between old and new Cleburne was dramatically demonstrated during the past year.

The incident that sparked the controversy was the death of the son of a prominent Cleburne family of an AIDS related disease. The citizens of Cleburne, while aware of the existence of AIDS, had not paid much attention until this unfortunate event. As a consequence of this death, the local newspaper, the *Cleburne Gazette*, began giving AIDS-related articles a more prominent position in its reporting. In one article, it was reported that the Cleburne Public School District was not in compliance with state regulations to implement an AIDS curriculum. A group of parents who read the article became concerned that their children were not being provided with necessary instruction about AIDS and AIDS prevention. This group of parents was mostly made up of Cleburne's new arrivals. This group petitioned the school board for time at their April meeting to discuss the implementation of an AIDS curriculum at Margaret Sanger High School.

The school district had successfully avoided this controversial issue because the increased numbers of new students and the problems associated with a rapidly growing student population had made implementation of an AIDS curriculum a low priority. Also, the district was unsure about how to approach the issue because of the community's strong and traditional bias against teaching any sex-related topic in the schools.

The request for time at the school board meeting was announced two weeks before the meeting in the *Gazette*. The community was immediately mobilized as two opposing camps prepared for the meeting. The *Gazette* sent an extra reporter to cover what was anticipated to be the most controversial meeting in the school board's history.

As expected, the meeting was tense and emotionally charged. Concerned parents stated their reasons for wanting an AIDS curriculum implemented during the next school year. A large coalition of conservative, long time community members attended the meeting to voice their concern about introducing AIDS education into the schools. Just as the tensions and voices began to be raised, the superintendent rose to speak. He said that while he personally agreed with the conservative coalition of parents, he was duty-bound to remind the group that AIDS education was required by state regulations.

After additional discussion, the superintendent rose again to speak. He announced that the Director of Secondary Education had gathered several examples of AIDS curricula that would provide the basis for selecting the AIDS curriculum at Margaret Sanger High School. In keeping with the district policy of school-based management, the selection of the appropriate AIDS curriculum would be made by the school's Curriculum Council. The Director of Secondary Education promised to provide the principal with the sample curricula and the State Curriculum Guidelines early next week. The Curriculum Council was charged with making a recommendation on an AIDS curriculum and reporting the rationale for their recommendation at the July meeting. The school board limited the time for review with the hope of implementing the chosen curriculum during the next school year since all of the publicity surrounding the school board meetings had alerted state officials about Cleburne's failure to comply with state regulations.

As members of the Curriculum Council for Margaret Sanger High School, you are charged to:

1. review the state guidelines, sample curricula, and any information you deem relevant
2. develop a recommendation and rationale for consideration by the superintendent and the Board of Education
3. prepare a presentation to the Board of Education for the July meeting at which you will present your recommendation and rationale

The board has allotted 45 minutes to this item on the agenda. Your presentation is scheduled for 2 p.m. on the final session of this project; it should last no more than 20 minutes.

The roles of the Curriculum Council should mirror the various constituents within the school community who would appropriately help make a curricular decision. When selecting both the roles and the curriculum, keep in mind the context in which the decision is being made. You will each be asked to discuss your role and the council's rationale for the curriculum being recommended at the July school board meeting.

School Board Member Profiles

Bradford Phillips, School Board President

Mr. Phillips is a member of one of the most prominent families in Cleburne. He is an attorney by profession, but devotes a great deal of time to community affairs. He has been a school board member for fifteen years, president for ten. Mr. Phillip's children are older and no longer attend Cleburne schools. Mr. Phillips is alarmed by the rapid changes to the Cleburne area due to the influx of new residents and is concerned that Cleburne's rural way of life is being destroyed.

Jimmy Hatfield, School Board Vice President

Mr. Hatfield has been a member of the school board for twenty years. He runs the local hardware store where long time Cleburne residents go to find the latest town information. Mr. Hatfield is well known for his genial, friendly demeanor and is quite popular with local children who he frequently takes along on hunting and fishing trips. Mr. Hatfield has no children in the local schools.

Darla Stewart, School Board Secretary

Mrs. Stewart was a second-grade teacher in the years before she began rearing a family. Her children are grown and Mrs. Stewart has devoted some of her considerable energies to various volunteer projects around Cleburne, including sitting on the school board for the past ten years. Mrs. Stewart is also active in her church, helps with a local literacy project, and runs the local food pantry.

Janine Hollis, School Board Member

Ms. Hollis is a highly successful real estate agent who is well known for her abilities as a dealmaker. She has one child at Margaret Sanger High School and has been a school board member for three years. She ran for election to the school board because she was concerned about the quality of her daughter's education. Ms. Hollis is also a life-long resident of Cleburne.

William Broderick, School Board Member

Mr. Broderick is the newest member of the board, having been elected to complete the term of Danny Robinson who died while in office. Mr. Broderick moved to the Cleburne area from the Northeast to manage the silicon wafer manufacturing facility. Mr. Broderick has one child in the local schools; another attends private school.

Rationale for Health Education

The need for education in all areas of health is greater today than ever before. The vitality, productivity, and longevity of Americans are now endangered by chronic diseases such as diabetes, cardiovascular conditions, and cancer. The incidence of these diseases depends, in large part, on choices people make each day—decisions on such things as exercise, diet, and the use of alcohol and drugs. There is currently great interest on the part of consumers in making informed choices—they want to know more and do more to keep healthy.

Health education is a means of enabling people to assume a greater role in their own health care. Health education in the schools, kindergarten through grade 12, can help children develop a positive attitude about health, can provide them with information on ways to take care of their health, and can help them acquire skills to make health-related decisions now and in the future.

Curriculum Guidelines

The purpose of these state guidelines is to provide school districts with the required topics of health education and to provide a framework from which a health education curriculum can be developed that meets the specific needs of each school district.

The purpose of health education is to help students reach their full educational potential through the understanding and practice of the principles of good physical and mental health. The following guidelines are designed to facilitate the accomplishment of this goal.

1. **Community Health**—Understanding the dependence of a community's health upon the health of all its citizens.

2. **Consumer Health**—Understanding the importance of wise de-cision-making in consumer health to the welfare of society.

3. **Disease Control**—Understanding the responsibility of indi-viduals for their own health and for the health of others.

4. **Environmental Health**—Understanding the relationship be-tween environmental influences and health conditions.

5. **Family Life**—Understanding the importance of interpersonal relationships and lifestyles to the quality of life.

6. **Mental Health**—Understanding factors involved in the devel-opment and maintenance of good mental health.

7. **Nutrition**—Understanding the importance of wise food choices and proper dietary habits to good health.

8. **Personal Health**—Understanding the dependence of wellness upon the maintenance of personal health.

9. **Safety and First Aid**—Understanding the importance of wise decision-making by individuals in controlling loss of lives, personal injury, and property damage.

10. **Substance Use and Abuse**—Understanding the proper and improper use of medicines and drugs.

Activities Guide

Unlike previous projects, each participant will be given a different article that discusses an issue associated with curriculum selection. The material contained in these articles may be useful to the team as a whole in deliberating on this curriculum decision and in preparing the final presentation. Each member will make a short presentation about his/her particular reading to the entire team. This will introduce the rest of the team to the material and give each member an opportunity to practice presentation skills.

Products

1. Individual presentation (5-8 minutes) that introduces the team to the material covered in the assigned article. (Do not merely summarize the material in the article. You need to indicate what the implications are for creating an AIDS curriculum and/or your presentation to the Board of Education. Submit a video-tape of your presentation.)

2. Prepare a video critique form that contains 4 or 5 items on which you desire feedback for your 8-minute individual pre-sentation. Submit the forms completed by the members of your

team. (See sample feedback forms in your resources for possible suggestions.)

3. A paper (7-page max) that describes:

    (a) the members of the Curriculum Council and why each member was included

    (b) an audience analysis of both the school board and likely attendees at the next school board meeting (Assume that a cross-section of the board will be present.)

    (c) the process and rationale for the curriculum recommendation, including the points of view of different team members/constituents

    (d) an assessment of whether the presentation at the board meeting achieved the desired results and a discussion of why the results did or did not match intentions

4. Videotaped presentation of the Curriculum Council's curriculum recommendation to the school board.

5. Please complete your "Talk Back" sheet and prepare an integrative essay (not to exceed two double-spaced typewritten pages) that reflects what you have learned during this project.

Resources

AIDS Information

Research on AIDS and Sex Education

"How Effective Is AIDS Education?" USDE publication.

J. Eckland. "Policy Choices for AIDS Education in the Public Schools." *Educational Evaluation and Policy Analysis* 11,4 (Winter 1989): 377-87.

C. Thomas. "Sex Education Is Failing Our Teens." *San Jose Mercury News,* October 7, 1990, p. 3C.

AIDS Curriculum (examples of approaches and materials)

Nashville AIDS Curriculum

New York State AIDS Curriculum

Lesson Plan(s) on AIDS

San Rafael (CA) City Schools AIDS curriculum

Diocese of Monterey (CA), HIV/ARC/AIDS Education

"A Letter from Brian," Red Cross Videotape

"The Los Altos Story," documentary on videotape of AIDS in a small, affluent community

"AIDS: Common Questions and Answers"

Policy Statements on AIDS Education

"Guidelines for Effective School Education to Prevent the Spread of AIDS," *MMWR,* 37 (January 29, 1988), S-2, 1-14. (U.S. Department of Health and Human Services.)

"Consensus Statement on AIDS in Schools," World Consultation of Teachers' International Organizations in association with: World Health Organization, United Nations Educational, Scientific and Cultural Organization, and International Labour Organisation.
Religious groups' policy statements on AIDS

Presentations

Persuasive
M. Berger. "Persuasive Presentations."

Informational/Explanatory
N. Gage and D. Berliner. "Lecturing and Explaining." In *Educational Psychology* (Fourth Edition). 396-428. Boston: Houghton Mifflin Company, 1988.

Feedback Forms
Form 11.8. Teacher Lectures, Presentations, and Demonstrations (Good and Brophy, *Looking in Classrooms*.)
Videotape Feedback Form.
[May use either of the above forms or use them as a basis for creating your own feedback form.]
General Presentation Information
Saving Face: Audience Analysis and the Successful Presentation
Hints for Successful Presenters

Curriculum Selection

Walker, D. "Curriculum Policy Making." *In Fundamentals of Curriculum*. 424-65. San Diego: Harcourt Brace Jovanovich, 1990.
Miller, J. *The Educational Spectrum: Orientations to Curriculum*. New York: Longman (1983). Pp. 9-32; 33-56; 57-82; 108-134; 135-159.
Doll, R. "Participants and Their Roles in Curriculum Improvement." Pp. 360-75.

General Case Information
Biographies of School Board Members for Cleburne Public Schools
Curriculum Guidelines and Rationale for Health Education

Assigned Articles
Note: Each person should prepare a 5-8 minute presentation to the project team based on one of the articles listed below. (See section on *Products* for additional information about this presentation.) The articles and assignments are as follows:

1. Miller, *Orientations to Curriculum*

   a. pp. 9-32 (Lyn)
   b. pp. 33-56 (Nicki)
   c. pp. 57-82 (Lupe)
   d. pp. 108-134 (Sal)
   e. pp. 135-159 (Paige)

[If you were assigned one of the articles listed above, you should read the article and select one of the perspectives discussed in it as the basis for your presentation.]

2. "How Effective Is AIDS Education?" USDE publication. (Kit)

TEACHER SELECTION

Introduction

T he context for creating and maintaining a quality teaching force is taking shape. Most districts will be hiring, rather than laying off, teachers. The supply is not expected to meet the demand, especially in the areas of math, science, and special education. If the pattern of the 60s, the period of the last teacher shortage, repeats itself, nearly half of the newly hired teachers will leave their districts within three years and the teaching profession within seven years. Moreover, the most talented are more likely to leave than the least talented. Those who stay are unlikely to lose their jobs for either marginal or poor performance.

If this is the context, how might administrators seek to create and maintain a quality teaching force? The answer to this important question is multifaceted. Administrators need to mount a comprehensive approach to the problem, one that addresses recruitment, selection, treatment of new hires, and granting tenure. Although this project emphasizes only one aspect of this approach, namely, selection, it is important for the prospective principal to consider these other issues as well.

The effectiveness of any selection process depends in part on the quantity and quality of the applicant pool. Hiring mistakes are much more likely when there is a high selection ratio (that is, the organization is forced to hire a relatively high proportion of the applicants). To increase the size and quality of the applicant pool, administrators should treat recruitment as a marketing problem. Marketing specialists identify the consumers' needs (in this instance, the applicant is a potential consumer) and then proceed to show how the product or service (in this instance, the district represents the product or service) will satisfy the consumers' needs. The marketing specialist also realizes that consumers will continue to buy the product or to use the service only if the product or service delivers on its promises.

Once the applicant is hired, the organization needs to create the conditions under which successful performance is likely. The quality of the teacher's performance is affected by several factors. The most obvious determinants are the teacher's competence and motivation.

Less obvious, but no less important, are the level of difficulty of the teacher's assignment, the level and type of support that the teacher receives, and the resources that the organization provides the teacher to carry out his/her role.

Unfortunately, most new hires do not teach under conditions that are conducive to success. Compared with the veterans on the staff, the newcomer often has more of everything—more preps, more rooms in which to teach, more students who are viewed as difficult to teach, and more extraclass responsibilities. Newcomers also have relatively fewer organizational resources to meet these demands. Veterans have accumulated instructional materials, supplies, and equipment over the years. They also have inherited resources from colleagues who have retired or moved on to other occupations. To maximize the possibility that newcomers will be effective and find their role satisfying, principals should strive to create more favorable working conditions for new hires. If newcomers are to succeed and to experience job satisfaction, they should receive an assignment with a reasonable level of difficulty, sufficient resources to meet the organization's demands, and ample substantive and social-emotional support. It is the principal's responsibility to create these conditions.

Even if the conditions are conducive to effective performance, the teacher may fail to meet the district's standards of performance. Hiring mistakes are inevitable because there are no fool-proof selection procedures or tools. The probationary period offers the principal an opportunity to identify these hiring mistakes and to verify whether the newcomer is a fully competent teacher who deserves tenure. It is virtually impossible for a district to create and maintain a quality teaching force unless these tenure decisions are sound ones.

Few principals relish the thought of having to make a negative tenure decision; they prefer to hire teachers who have the right stuff. Principals are in a much better position to improve their ratio of hits to misses if they are familiar with what research has to say about the reliability and validity of the various selection tools. They also are more likely to make a sound hiring decision if they can overcome the basic human tendency to focus on individual behavior and to ignore the context in which this behavior was observed.

The importance of this dual concern for behavior and context became evident when I recently served as a consultant to a local school district that was interested in improving its hiring process. This district had hired a teacher who was exceptional with honors students but a failure with less talented students. Upon examining the teacher's recommendations, we discovered that she had received a superb evaluation from her student teaching supervisor. The supervisor had observed her teaching only one type of student—the academically gifted and talented. Although the applicant had taught remedial classes as well, there was no evaluation of her performance in this context. One cannot assume that a person who teaches well in one situation will perform well in a quite different context unless the person has been observed and evaluated in both contexts.

In designing the selection process, principals need to realize that they are attempting to predict how an applicant will behave in a particular context. The accuracy of this prediction is likely to be greater if two conditions are met. First, the selection process is structured to elicit the kinds of behavior that one is trying to predict. Second, the context in which the behavior is being observed resembles the context in which the person will subsequently perform. As you read about the soundness of various selection tools and contemplate how you will design your own teacher selection process, bear these two conditions in mind.

Principals also need to realize that the selection process entails a choice by the applicant, as well as the organization. Individuals who are treated poorly during the recruitment and selection phase are apt to decline an offer of employment. To reduce the incidence of backouts, principals should structure the recruitment and selection process in a way that reflects a concern for the individual (for example, prompt and nonbureaucratic responses to inquiries, reasonable speed in making decisions, and timely information about what has happened or is happening with the individual's application). Moreover, the offer of employment should be personalized and exhibit a willingness to assist the individual in making the transition to the school and the community.

Learning Objectives

This project has been designed to provide you with an opportunity to learn about the following issues:

1. selection tools and what research has to say about each of these tools

2. the design and implementation of protocols for using the various selection tools

3. the legal aspects of teacher selection

Guiding Questions

1. What is the information that you will be seeking? Why have you chosen to gather this information? How will you be gathering it?

2. Is it reasonable to expect the selection tool to yield this information?

3. Which selection tools seem to be the *most defensible* in light of research? *least defensible?*

4. What are some of the purposes, other than choosing the person with the right stuff, for which the interview and the work sample might be used?

5. What are the legal aspects of selection that may enter into this project?

6. What does the principal need to know about the legal aspects of misassignment in California?

Problem (high school version)

Assume that the Mountain View-Los Altos High School District is looking for an English teacher and that you have been appointed to the Selection Committee. One individual will serve as the chair of the selection committee. The tasks of the selection committee are as follows:

- *Read the background information*

  1. The Certificated Position announcement

  2. The description of the policy context and the teacher evaluation system in MV-LA

  3. The criteria for teaching effectiveness used by the MV-LA school district

- *Create an application blank that you will use for this position.* This application blank should be legally defensible and should solicit information that you will use in evaluating the suitability of applicants for the position. Attach to the application blank your rationale for the information that you are requesting.

- *Design the interview and work sample that you will use*

  District policy requires that selection committees use two methods—a work sample (involves teaching a lesson) and an interview. Spell out the details of the procedures your committee will follow when implementing each method and explain why you intend to use these procedures. Be sure that your procedures are legally defensible.

- *Implement your procedures*

  Use the interview and work sample that you have designed to choose the person whom you will recommend for the position. Three individuals have volunteered to participate in the selection process as "applicants." We will supply the names and phone numbers of these individuals; you will need to make all the necessary arrangements.

* *Notify each "applicant" of the outcome*

As a condition of participating in this simulation, each volunteer wants to know whether (s)he was selected and what suggestions your committee might have for helping the person to improve.

Product Specifications

Your selection committee is expected to provide a report (not to exceed one page, single spaced) to the Director of Personnel. (NOTE: Use the reader-centered and PM approaches that you were introduced to in the *Write Right!* project when preparing this report.) This report should contain the following:

1. the recommendation of your committee

2. an overview of the selection process that you used

3. a justification for your recommendation

4. what should be done to ensure the candidate's success once hired

Attach to this report a copy of the application blank (including the rationale behind it) you created, the questions you asked during the interview, the work sample guidelines you gave the applicants, and any other materials your committee may have created during the selection process.

You will also be expected to provide each volunteer with the following information: (a) the outcome (Is the person being recommended for the position?) and (b) feedback regarding perceived strengths and areas in need of improvement. This information may be communicated face-to-face or in writing. (If you put the information in writing, provide me with a copy.)

Assessment

Complete the "Knowledge Review Exercise on the Legal Aspects of Teacher Selection."

When you have finished the "Knowledge Review" and your product, please prepare an integrative essay (not to exceed two typewritten, double-spaced pages) that reflects what you have learned while completing this project. Also, fill out the *Talk Back* Sheet.

Turn in the product, the "Knowledge Review," the essay, and the *Talk Back* sheet by the dates specified on the course calendar.

Resources

RECRUITMENT

Ryans, S. "The Employment Interview as a Recruitment Device." In *The Employment Interview: Theory, Research and Practice*, edited by R. Eder and G. Ferris. 127-41. Beverly Hills, CA: Sage Publications, Inc., 1989.

SELECTION

Legal aspects

Duffy, D. "Defamation and Employer Privilege." *Employee Relations Law Journal* 9 (3): 444-54.

Tidwell, J. "Educators' Liability for Negative Letters of Recommendation." *Journal of Law and Education* 15 4 (Fall 1986): 479-83.

———. "The New Rules for Interviewing Job Applicants: Schools Ignore Them at Their Peril." *American School Board Journal*, (March 1977): 27-30.

Research

Goodale, J. "Effective Employment Interviewing." In *The Employment Interview: Theory, Research and Practice*, edited by R. Eder and G. Ferris. 307-23. Beverly Hills, CA: Sage Publications, Inc., 1989. [Strongly recommended.]

LeTendre B. "The Use of Work Samples in the Hiring Process." 1989. Pp. 157-61; 224-48; 277-78; and 280-81. [Strongly recommended.]

Muchinsky, P. "The Use of Reference Reports in Personnel Selection." *Journal of Occupational Psychology* 52 (1979): 287-97.

Robertson, I., and Kandola, R. "Work Sample Tests: Validity, Adverse Impact, and Applicant Reaction." *Journal of Occupational Psychology* 55 (1982): 171-83.

Schalock, D. "Research on Teacher Selection." In *Review of Research in Education* 7 (1979): 389-417.

Wise, A., and others. *Effective Teacher Selection*. Santa Monica, CA: Rand Corporation, 1987. Pp. 1-11.

DUTIES OF A TEACHER

Scriven, M. "Duties of the Teacher." (Mimeographed, 1990.). Pp. 1-11. [Strongly recommended.]

TREATMENT OF NEW HIRES

Support for New Teachers

Kass, M., and others. *Building the Future: Making a Difference for Beginning Teachers*. Chapter 1: "Support for New Teachers," 1990. Pp. 1-1 to 1-10. [Strongly recommended.]

Misassignment

Video on misassignment produced by State Department of Education.

Commission on Teacher Credentialing, State of California (1987). *Teacher Assignment Practices in California School Districts: A Report to the California State Legislature*.

Commission on Teacher Credentialing, State of California (1988). *The Administrator's Assignment Manual*. (Become familiar with contents and use.)

IN ENGLISH, PLEASE

The United States of America is a nation of immigrants, and the state of California epitomizes the linguistic, ethnic, and cultural diversity that accompanies immigration. In 1990 slightly more than half of the 29,760,021 residents were white. Hispanics accounted for 26 percent of the population; Asians and Pacific Islanders for another 9 percent; African-Americans amounted to 7 percent; and American Indians, Eskimos, and Aleutians for nearly 1 percent. This diversity, as in previous periods of our history, poses a formidable challenge for the public schools in California and elsewhere.

One of the major challenges facing the schools is how to deal effectively with students who lack proficiency in the English language. In California one of every seven students is either Non-English Proficient (NEP) or Limited English Proficient (LEP). Although most of these NEP and LEP students attend the early grades, they are also to be found in the upper grades. Helping these children to communicate and to learn in English represents a major goal and challenge for the schools.

Despite virtually unanimous agreement on the goal, there is considerable disagreement about how the goal should be attained. The underlying issues are complex, often misunderstood, and frequently charged with great emotion. The principal stakeholders in these issues have sought their resolution in a variety of forums: the schools, the state legislature, the U. S. Congress, the court room, and the ballot box. Despite these efforts, the issues remain unsettled and the center of heated disputes.

Scholars and researchers have sought to shed light on these issues and to identify effective teaching strategies and programs for helping NEP and LEP students to acquire proficiency in the English language. Although the theoretical and empirical work of these scholars points to effective and ineffective ways of acquiring proficiency in a second language, the public and educators alike continue to harbor misconceptions about these programs. In consequence, they unwittingly perpetuate policies, programs, and practices that exacerbate rather than solve the problem.

In this problem-based learning project, you will be introduced to a number of the issues surrounding America's multilingual past. At the same time you will learn about the research and theory that bear on these issues. In addition you will become knowledgeable about the legal and fiscal aspects of providing an education for NEP and LEP students who are striving to acquire proficiency in English as a second language.

Learning Objectives

1. Acquire knowledge and understanding of the major issues that confront a school serving a linguistically diverse population

2. Obtain insight into the various approaches that might be used to deal with these issues

3. Acquire knowledge and understanding of the theory and research that relate to these issues and approaches

4. Become knowledgeable about the legal aspects of providing an education for a linguistically diverse student population

5. Develop a personal philosophy/rationale about bilingual education that can be communicated to a diverse audience

Guiding Questions

1. In what respects is the King Middle School in and out of compliance with state and federal laws governing the education of linguistically diverse populations?

2. The letter from Mrs. Olson contains a number of opinions and perceptions? Which of these are unfounded (i.e., inconsistent with what research has to say about the education and linguistic practices of those for whom English is a second language)?

3. What are the existing resources within the district and the school that might be used to enhance the education of this linguistically diverse population, how are they currently being deployed (including proposals for deployment), and how might they be re-deployed?

4. What approaches might be used to provide an education for this linguistically diverse population?

5. What approach(es) would you favor, and how would you defend your choice?

Problem

Read the case, *In English, Please!*

Product Specifications

As the first-year principal of King Middle School, you have decided to appoint a Bilingual Advisory Committee consisting of yourself, parents with opposing views (English only, second generation Hispanic, recent Hispanic immigrant, and non-Hispanic), and teachers (intermediate, upper grade, and bilingual). Prior to the first meeting, you intend to circulate a packet of materials that you have prepared. This packet should contain the following materials:

(a) a statement that describes the committee's charge

(b) a tentative plan for how the committee should proceed to accomplish its charge

(c) an agenda for the meeting that clarifies what the content and the process will be for the meeting

(d) a statement (not to exceed two single-spaced typewritten pages) that attempts to provide committee members with the background information that you believe all committee members should have about bilingual education

(e) a statement (not to exceed one single-spaced typewritten page) that discusses what your current views on bilingual education are

[**Note:** In wrestling with the issues in this case you may find that it does not contain some crucial information you need. In this event, make whatever assumptions you feel are reasonable in light of the other facts presented in the case. Make these assumptions explicit.]

Assessment

When you have finished your product, please prepare an integrative essay that reflects what you have learned while completing this project. Also, complete the *Talk Back* sheet.

Resources

Readings
BILINGUAL EDUCATION

THEORY
Schooling and Language Minority Students: A Theoretical Framework, 1981. Pp. 3-146. [Strongly recommended.]
Glossary of Terms for Bilingual Education in *Schooling and Language Minority Students*. Pp. 215-18.

RESEARCH
"Basic Research on Language Acquisition." In Crawford, 1989. Pp. 97-111. [Strongly recommended.]
THEORY INTO PRACTICE
"Theory into Practice: The Case Studies Project." In Crawford, 1989. Pp. 126-41. [Strongly recommended.]
R. Porter. "The Newton Alternative to Bilingual Education." *The Annals of the American Academy of Political and Social Science* (March 1990). Pp. 147-59.
S. Morison. "A Spanish-English Dual-Language Program in New York City." *The Annals* (March 1990): Pp. 160-69.

POLICY
"Bilingual Education: Learning English." *EdSource* XI (January 1988): Pp. 1-8.
"Final Report of the Bilingual Education Task Force" (One example of a school district policy on bilingual education). Redwood City School District, Redwood City, CA, June 6, 1990.

HISTORICAL CONTEXT
J. Perlman. "Historical Legacies: 1840-1920." *The Annals of the American Academy of Political and Social Science* (March 1990). Pp. 27-37. [Strongly recommended.]

LEGAL CONTEXT
B. Piatt, "Language Rights in the Classroom." In *Only English?* Albuquerque, New Mexico: University of New Mexico Press, 1990. Pp. 37-57.
"State Requirements for Programs Serving Limited English Proficient Students" (CCR document containing compliance items). Mimeographed, undated but current. [Strongly recommended.]

THE ENGLISH-ONLY MOVEMENT
A. Padilla, and others. "The English-Only Movement: Myths, Reality and Implications for Psychology." *Journal of the American Psychological Association* 46,1 (February 1991): 121-30. [Strongly recommended.]

MANAGING ADVISORY COMMITTEES (TASK FORCES)
J. Ware. *Managing a Task Force*. Boston, Massachusetts: Soldiers Field, Harvard Business School, 1977.
E. Bridges. "Notes on a Prescription for Consensus Building in Ad Hoc Groups" (Task Forces), 1991. (Mimeographed.)

In English, Please!

You are in your first year as principal of the King Middle School. At this point you are wondering whether your decision to become a principal was a wise one. You fully expected to make a difference and were eager to confront the challenges facing public education. Now, these challenges seem overwhelming.

A troubling issue sits on your desk. Mrs. Lorie Olsen, the leader of a group of concerned parents, has written you a letter about the "Hispanic problem" at the school. For the third time you begin to read this letter from her.

Dear Principal Smith:

I was listening to the radio yesterday and heard a well known commentator discussing an issue that concerns our group. His concern, like ours, is the promotion and use of other languages by so many in our country who do not appear to be attempting to learn English or become part of the melting pot. He equated the problems here with those in Quebec, and warned that with our policies the time would come when we would have states seceding from our union.

The problems involved with non-English speaking students has long been a challenge for our school system. Every public agency in the state is burdened with providing interpreters and often literature in several different languages, especially Spanish. The cost of these services is astronomical. Perhaps, if there was a happy ending to the story it would not be so perturbing. But, year after year, these same people continue to expect the United States to support their lack of language acquisition—and on and on indefinitely. States like California never get ahead because a new wave enters the system daily without an equal number exiting.

Now this problem is starting to plague our school. Our concern is with the large numbers of such people who bleed all sorts of funding agencies, and generation after generation, never do learn English. The parents never read English books, never watch English television and never attempt to speak English. Their children are cut from the same cloth; the only place they try to speak English is at school. Our experience tells us that these kids eventually wind up costing the system lots of money, money better spent on kids who come to school to learn and are capable of doing so. We already spend too much money on special education services. Before long these kids from across the border will be classified as "learning disabled" and receive more attention than kids who are serious about their education.

Let's quit paying translators and expect these people to provide their own. Let's quit printing tests for drivers licenses, school notices, etc. in several different languages and let these people either learn to read English or provide their own assistance. Cruel? We think not. Didn't your ancestors have to learn English to found this country? Ours did.

Our democratic government is based on an informed electorate. Unless one can read, write, and speak the language of the country, how can he or she truly know and understand the issues and be adequately informed?

We believe the key is motivation. If these people weren't fed, clothed, housed and given medical assistance so freely perhaps the motivation would be there to learn English and find jobs.

Granted there are no easy solutions but we need to begin moving toward the goal of expecting people to speak English. It would save a fortune in salaries and services and in the long run reduce unemployment because these people could find jobs and get off welfare. Test scores would rise, and the need for special classes would be reduced.

While you are trying to find a solution for this problem, we want you to put these kids in separate classes. There's no law that says these kids must sit side by side with children who come to school ready and able to learn. Other schools have tracking. It works there, and there is no reason why it won't work here.

You have our views on this problem. We await a letter or phone call from you—in English please!

 Sincerely,

Mrs. Lorie Olsen, President

Concerned Parents Group

You put the letter down again and say to yourself:

As if that isn't bad enough, many of the teachers are also complaining. The complaints are pretty consistent: "It's impossible to teach these kids. The district keeps raising class size. At the same time they're sending us more and more kids who don't understand English and don't seem motivated to learn it. If the truth be known, they probably don't know their own language all that well and weren't doing all that well in school even if they were going to school which they probably weren't. It's unreasonable to expect us to deal effectively with this situation. We don't have the skills to teach these kinds. Our ESL program isn't working either. These kids are pulled out of our class for 20 minutes a day and don't show any improvement. If a bilingual aide can't accomplish anything, how do you expect us to?"

Moments later your mind flashes back to a conversation you had two days ago with a leader in the Hispanic community. He was quite reasonable but very forthright about the problems at King. The gist of his comments as you recall was as follows:

The school is a tinder box ready to be ignited at any minute. Students don't like coming to school. They feel unwelcome. They sense that the teachers don't understand them and are not making much of an effort to help the students adjust to a foreign environment or succeed in school. Most teachers ignore the students' cultural heritage and discourage them from ever saying anything in their native language. There isn't anything in their classes that students can relate to; everything seems so different from what things were like in their homeland. The Anglo students resent the presence of Hispanics and harrass, tease, and intimidate them daily. Overt racial conflict will break out any day if racial relations don't improve.

Many of the Hispanic parents are not well educated and are reluctant to come to school because they don't speak English very well. First generation immigrant parents also distrust authorities and prefer to remain invisible because they don't know their legal rights and fear that they might be deported. These parents also are pretty confused about the American school system and are inclined to believe that school officials and teachers know what's best for their children. Second generation immigrant parents feel that their children are being treated badly here at King, are angry about it but don't know what to do. If something isn't done and racial conflict erupts in the school, you won't be able to count on any support or cooperation from any of the Hispanic parents, first or second generation.

You also must realize that Hispanic parents have needs of their own that aren't being met. Some want to learn how to read and write, either in English or in Spanish. Others desire to help their children with their homework. Still others want to be informed about school issues, to receive help and guidance in raising their children, and to know what their legal rights are. If you really want the cooperation of these parents, you should address their needs, as well as their children's.

Adding to your problems is the lack of credentialed bilingual teachers and the district assignment policies that have been negotiated with the teachers' union. Assignment preference goes to senior teachers, regardless of the special needs of individual schools. Given the number of Hispanic students in your school, you should have more teachers with bilingual certification. However, they just aren't available, and your school is out of compliance with the law. You wonder what that portends for the future. Perhaps, you could avoid the legal problems by supporting the district's proposal to establish a newcomers' center for Hispanics. This proposal (see attached) is currently under consideration by the Superintendent's cabinet to which you belong.

Meanwhile....

Proposed Newcomer Center for Hispanic Students

The Baylands Elementary School District is currently considering a proposal to establish a Newcomer Center for Hispanic Students. This center will focus on students in grades 4-8 and will be funded through the federal Emergency Immigrant Education Assistance Program and district funds. Students who speak limited or no English will be assigned to the Newcomer Center for a period not to exceed six months. The center will have four major functions:

1. to provide comprehensive assessment services
2. to conduct physical examinations
3. to provide a transitional educational program
4. to orient parents of the new students to the Baylands Schools, the American educational system, and broader issues about American life

Comprehensive assessment services. These new students will be assessed through five exams in (a) oral primary language use and comprehension, (b) English reading, (c) English writing, (d) mathematics, and (e) tests in Spanish to ascertain native language literacy levels. Two bilingual specialists will conduct these assessments.

Physical examinations. In addition to academic assessment, the center will provide physical health examinations to students. One full-time nurse-practitioner will be assigned to carry out these duties at the center.

Transitional educational program. Students may stay up to six months and receive intensive ESL instruction in oral language, reading and life skills, PE, general math, and world cultural studies. There will be five teachers (all bilingual in Spanish and English) assigned full-time to the center.

Services to parents of student newcomers. An orientation handbook will be made available in Spanish for parents and students. This handbook will contain basic information about school services, graduation requirements, expectations, how to obtain a locker and lunch tickets, and contacts for further assistance. In addition, the center will develop and show a slide show about the schools, with audiocassettes in Spanish, for use at quarterly orientation meetings for newly arrived parents and weekly sessions for students. The parent meetings will also include information about the schools and broader issues as well, including health, employment, immigration, and parental involvement in education. The center will build a network of community agencies to work with parents on these issues.

Other staff of the center will include a full-time coordinator and secretary. The center coordinator will work with school principals and receiving teachers to ensure that students receive transitional support when they are assigned to regular classrooms.

Estimated costs for the center during its first year of operation will be approximately $275,000.

Fact Sheet: King Middle School (4-8)

Enrollment: 950 [327 Hispanic (100 LEP), 30 Black, and 593 White]

Staff

Principal
Assistant Principal
Two counselors
Nurse
41 teachers (2 credentialed bilingual; should have 10)
4 bilingual aides

Curricular and Instructional Program

8th Grade—2-period core featuring language arts and reading
7th Grade—3-period core featuring language arts, reading, and social studies
4th, 5th, 6th, 7th, and 8th Grade—pullout program, 20 minutes daily, for ESL students
6th Grade—dual 3-period core schedule
Interdisciplinary teaming
Team teaching
7-period day
Elective and exploratory classes
4th and 5th grades are self-contained

Extracurricular Program

Student Activity Center
After school sports and recreation
Performing arts (band and chorus)

Parent/Community Involvement

PTA
School Site Council
(Virtually no participation of Hispanic parents)

Student suspensions

226 days of suspension during the previous year
81 different students suspended

Students suspended for these reasons in order of occurrence: Fighting (by far the leading reason), defiance or insubordination, alcohol/drugs, vandalism, and smoking

Test Information

On statewide tests, King scored at the 50th percentile last year compared to other schools in the state that serve students with similar backgrounds.

(**Note**: The Baylands School District has six elementary schools and two middle schools, including King.)

Project Checklist

[Project:_____]

___	1. VCR
___	2. TV monitor
___	3. Blank videotape
___	4. Videocamera
___	5. Easel
___	6. Butcher paper
___	7. Color marking pens
___	8. Chalk or erasable marking pens
___	9. Scotch tape or masking tape
___	10. Typewriter or computer
___	11. Printer
___	12. Access to copy machine
___	13. Office with phone and desk
___	14. Work table
___	15. Chalkboard
___	16. Instructional tape(s)
___	17. Original copy of each reading
___	18. Readings photocopied
___	19. Human resources needed _____
	_____
	_____
___	20. Answer key
___	21. Other: _____
	_____

Bibliography

Many of the items in this bibliography are indexed in ERIC's monthly catalog *Resources in Education (RIE)*. Reports in *RIE* are indicated by an "ED" number. Journal articles, indexed in ERIC's companion catalog, *Current Index to Journals in Education*, are indicated by an "EJ" number.

Most items with an ED number are available from ERIC Document Reproduction Service (EDRS), 7420 Fullerton Rd., Suite 110, Springfield, VA 22153-2852.

To order from EDRS, specify the ED number, type of reproduction desired—microfiche (MF) or paper copy (PC), and number of copies. Add postage to the cost of all orders and include check or money order payable to EDRS. For credit card orders, call 1-800-443-3742.

Acheson, Keith, and Meredith Gall. *Techniques in the Clinical Supervision of Teachers.* New York: Longman, 1987. 225 pages.

Barrows, H. "A Specific Problem-Based, Self-Directed Learning Method Designed to Teach Medical Problem-Solving Skills and Enhance Knowledge Retention." In *Tutorials in Problem-Based Learning*, edited by H. Schmidt and M. deVolder. 16-32. Maastricht, Netherlands: Van Gorcum, 1984.

Bok, D. "Needed: A New Way to Train Doctors." In *New Directions for Medical Education*, edited by H. Schmidt and others. 17-38. New York: Springer-Verlag, 1989.

Bransford, John; J. Franks; N. Vye; and R. Sherwood. "New Approaches to Instruction: Because Wisdom Can't Be Told." In *Similarity and Analogi-*

cal Reasonings, edited by Stella Vosniadou and Andrew Ortony. 470-97. New York: Cambridge University Press, 1989.

Bransford, John, and others. "Teaching Thinking and Problem Solving." *American Psychologist* 41, 10 (October 1986): 1078-89. EJ 360 275.

Bransford, John, and Barry Stein. *The IDEAL Problem Solver: A Guide for Improving Thinking, Learning, and Creativity*. New York: W.H. Freeman and Company, 1984. 150 pages.

Bridges, Edwin. "The Nature of Leadership." In *Educational Administration: The Developing Decades*, edited by Luvern Cunningham, Walter Hack, and Raphael Nystrand. Berkeley, California: McCutchan Publishing Corporation, 1977. 445 pages.

_____. "Combining Theory, Research and Practice: Problem-Based Learning." Paper presented at the University Council for Educational Administration Convention, October 27-29, 1989.

Burke, Kenneth. *Permanence and Change*. New York: New Republic, 1935.

Charters, W., and J. Jones. "On the Neglect of the Independent Variable in Program Evaluation." In *Managing Change in Educational Organizations: Sociological Perspectives, Strategies, and other Case Studies*, edited by J. Victor Baldridge and Terrance Deal. Berkeley, California: McCutchan, 1975. 523 pages.

Christensen, C.; D. Garvin; and A. Sweet. *Education for Judgment*. Boston: Harvard Business School, 1991.

Christensen, C. Roland, with Abby J. Hansen. *Teaching and the Case Method: Text, Cases, and Readings*. Boston: Harvard Business School, 1987.

Claessen, H., and H. Boshuizen. "Recall of Medical Information by Students and Doctors." *Medical Education* 19 (1985): 61-67.

Coles, C. "Differences between Conventional and Problem-Based Curricula in Their Students' Approaches to Studying." *Medical Education* 19 (1985): 308-9.

deVolder, M., and W. deGrave. "Approaches to Learning in a Problem-Based Medical Programme: A Developmental Study." *Medical Education* 23 (1989): 262-64.

deVries, M.; H. Schmidt; and E. deGraaff. "Dutch Comparisons: Cognitive and Motivational Effects of Problem-Based Learning on Medical Students." In *New Directions for Medical Education*, edited by H. Schmidt and others. 231-38. New York: Springer-Verlag, 1989.

Getzels, J. "Creative Administration and Organizational Change." In *Frontiers in School Leadership*, edited by L. Rubin. Chicago: Rand McNally and Company, Inc., 1970.

Godden, D., and A. Baddeley. "Context-Dependent Memory in Two Natural Environments: On Land and Underwater." *British Journal of Psychology* 66 (1975): 325-32.

Good, Thomas, and Jere Brophy. *Looking in Classrooms*. New York: Harper & Row, 1991.

Hallinger, Philip, and others. "Using a Problem-Based Approach for Instructional Leadership Development." *Journal of Staff Development* 12, 2 (Spring 1991): 6-12.

Harvey, J., and others. "Ranking Clinical Problems and Ocular Diseases in Ophthalmology: An Innovative Approach to Curricular Design." *Can J Ophthalmol* 23, 6 (1988): 255-58.

Hertenstein, J. "Patterns of Participation. " In *Education for Judgment*, edited by C. Christensen, D. Garvin, and A. Sweet. Boston: Harvard Business School Press, 1991.

Imbos, T., and others. "The Growth in Knowledge of Anatomy in a Problem-Based Curriculum." In *Tutorials in Problem-Based Learning*, edited by H. Schmidt and M. deVolder. 106-15. Maastricht, Netherlands: Van Gorcum, 1984.

Janis, I., and L. Mann. *Decision Making*. New York: The Free Press, 1977.

Jonas, H.; S. Etzel; and B. Barzansky. "Undergraduate Medical Education." *JAMA* 262, 8 (August 25, 1989): 1011-19.

Jones, J., and others. "A Problem-Based Curriculum—Ten Years of Experience." In *Tutorials in Problem-Based Learning*, edited by H. Schmidt and M. deVolder. 181-98. Maastricht, Netherlands: Van Gorcum, 1984.

Kaufman, A. *Implementing Problem-Based Medical Education*. New York: Springer Publishing Company, 1985.

Kaufman, A., and others. "The New Mexico Experiment: Educational Innovation and Institutional Change." *Academic Medicine* (June 1989 Supplement): 285-94.

Lloyd, J., and S. Abrahamson. "Effectiveness of Continuing Medical Education: A Review of the Evidence." *Evaluation and the Health Professions* 2, 3 (September 1979): 251-80.

Maddison, D. "What's Wrong with Medical Education?" *Medical Education*, 12 (1978): 97-102.

Manning, P., and L. DeBakey. *Medicine: Preserving the Passion*. New York: Springer-Verlag, 1987.

McGuire, Christine. "Assessment of Problem-Solving Skills, 2." *Medical Teacher* 2, 3 (1980): 118-22.

_____. "Medical Problem-Solving: A Critique of the Literature." *Journal of Medical Education* 60, 8 (August 1985): 587-95. EJ 323 916.

Mennin, S., and N. Martinez-Burrola. "The Cost of Problem-Based vs. Traditional Medical Education." *Medical Education* 20 (1986): 187-94.

Mitchell, G. "Problem-Based Learning in Medical Schools: A New Approach." *Medical Teacher* 10, 1 (1988): 57-67.

Newble, I., and R. Clarke. "The Approaches to Learning of Students in a Traditional and an Innovative Problem-Based Medical School." *Medical Education* 20 (1986): 267-73.

Prawat, Richard. "Promoting Access to Knowledge, Strategies, and Disposition in Students: A Research Synthesis." *Review of Educational Research* 59, 1 (Spring 1989): 1-41. EJ 399 812.

Saunders, K.; D. Northup; and S. Mennin. "The Library in a Problem-Based Curriculum." In *Implementing Problem-Based Medical Education,* edited by A. Kaufman. 71-88. New York: Springer Publishing Company, 1985.

Schmidt, H. "Problem-Based Learning: Rationale and Description." *Medical Education* 17 (1983): 11-16.

Schmidt, H.; W. Dauphinee; and V. Patel. "Comparing the Effects of Problem-based and Conventional Curricula in an International Sample." *Journal of Medical Education* 62 (April 1987): 305-15.

Schmidt, H., and M. deVolder. *Tutorials in Problem-Based Learning.* Maastricht, Netherlands: Van Gorcum, 1984.

Schmidt, H., and others. *New Directions for Medical Education.* New York: Springer-Verlag, 1989.

Schmidt, H. , and others. "Comparing the Effects of Problem-Based and Conventional Curricula in an International Sample." *Journal of Medical Education* 62, 4 (April 1987): 305-15. EJ 354 233.

Shahabudin, S. "Content Coverage in Problem-Based Learning." *Medical Education* 21 (1987): 310-13.

Walton, H., and M. Matthews. "Essentials of Problem-Based Learning." *Medical Education* 23 (1989): 542-58.

Waterman, R.; P. Akmajian; and S. Kearny. *Community-Oriented Problem-Based Learning at the University of New Mexico.* Albuquerque, New Mexico: University of New Mexico School of Medicine, 1991.

Waterman, R., and C. Butler. "Curriculum: Problems to Stimulate Learning." In *Implementing Problem-Based Medical Education,* edited by A. Kaufman. 16-44. New York: Spring Publishing Company, 1985.

Waterman, R.; S. Duban; S. Mennin; and A. Kaufman. *Clinical Problem-Based Learning.* Albuquerque, New Mexico: University of New Mexico Press, 1988.

Wilkerson, LuAnn, and Joseph Maxwell. "A Qualitative Study of Initial Faculty Tutors in a Problem-Based Curriculum." *Journal of Medical Education* 63 (December 1988): 892-99.

Willems, J. "Problem-Based (Group) Teaching: A Cognitive Science Approach to Using Available Knowledge." *Instructional Science* 10 (1981): 5-21.